Mind Your Own *Business!*

Getting Started as an *Entrepreneur*

La Verne Ludden Ed.D
&
Bonnie Maitlen, Ed.D.

It seems obvious that, if you were to start your own business, the risks might be high. But if it were easy, everyone else would do it. Right? So, to avoid your blaming us later should your decisions not work out, our friendly legal counsel suggested that we state the following paragraph. Please read it. On the other hand, should this book help you launch a successful venture, our editorial staff would most appreciate your sending tokens of your appreciation to us through the publisher, whose address is on this very page.

Caveat emptor . . . This book is sold as is, without warranty of any kind, either express or implied, respecting the contents of this book, including but not limited to implied warranties for the book's quality, performance, merchantability, or fitness for any purpose. This book is sold also with the understanding that the publisher and the authors are not engaged in rendering legal, accounting, or other professional services. Because this book is not offered, and should not be used, as a substitute for competent legal advice, the reader is advised to consult legal counsel regarding any points of law. Neither JIST Works, Inc., nor its authors, dealers, or distributors shall be liable to the purchaser or any other person or entity with respect to any liability, loss, or damage caused or alleged to be caused directly or indirectly by this book.

Publisher: J. Michael Farr
Project Director: Spring Dawn Reader
Editor: David Noble
Cover Design: Robert Steven Pawlak
Interior Design: Jinny Bastianelli
Composition/Layout: Carolyn J. Newland

Mind Your Own Business—Getting Started as an Entrepreneur

©1994, **JIST Works, Inc.**, Indianapolis, IN   Printed in the United States.

99 98   9 8 7 6 5 4

Send all inquiries to:
JIST Works, Inc.
720 North Park Avenue • Indianapolis, IN 46202-3431
Phone: **(317) 264-3720** • FAX: **(317) 264-3709**

Library of Congress Cataloging-in-Publication Data
Ludden, LaVerne, 1949-
  Mind Your Own Business! : Getting Started as an Entrepreneur /
LaVerne Ludden & Bonnie Maitlen.
      p.   cm.
  Includes bibliographical references and index.
  ISBN 1-56370-083-2 : $9.95
    1. New business enterprises—United States—Handbooks, manuals,
etc.   2. Small business—United States—Management—Handbooks,
manuals, etc.   I. Maitlen, Bonnie, 1950-   . II. Title.
HD62.5.L83   1993   93-6007
ISBN: 1-56370-083-2   CIP

To my wife, Marsha, and sons Chris, Matt, and Tim, who have been understanding and supportive throughout all my business endeavors.

—LaVerne

To my father, Glenn H. Shakley, who taught me the value of setting goals, believing in myself, and sharing with others what I have learned.

—Bonnie

Table of Contents

Introduction

Much of the current literature about entrepreneurs uses the words *self-employment* and *entrepreneurship* interchangeably. A distinction might be that an entrepreneur often looks for an opportunity for financial growth and seeks to achieve certain business goals. An individual who pursues self-employment might do so for a variety of reasons, including the achievement of a flexible schedule. Because the distinction between self-employment and entrepreneurship becomes quite blurred at times, the two terms are used interchangeably throughout this book.

In this book, you learn the basics of how to create and operate a successful new enterprise. These basics include the following tasks:

1. Deciding whether to start your own business
2. Selecting the right legal structure for your business
3. Preparing a business plan
4. Financing your business
5. Choosing a business team

Mind Your Own Business! is not meant to replace more detailed books about starting a business. However, this book provides a good foundation for launching a new enterprise. The book is intended to help you decide whether self-employment is an appropriate choice for you. As a workbook, *Mind Your Own Business!* provides an opportunity for you to respond to specific issues regarding self-employment. Through structured questions and checklists, you can record your responses in this workbook, generating a log and initiating steps toward your goal of becoming self-employed.

This workbook is another resource to be used by the would-be entrepreneur and is designed to help you learn more about self-employment. Chapter 1 reviews the challenges faced by an entrepreneur and sources that can provide you with assistance in creating and operating a business. In chapter 2, you learn about the characteristics and skills of entrepreneurs and determine how well these describe you. In chapter 3, you learn about how to start a business and avoid some of the common problems faced by inexperienced entrepreneurs. Chapters 4 to 8 provide information on writing a business plan, obtaining financing, developing a business team, and setting up an office. Because consulting is a form of self-employment that attracts many people, the final chapter is about becoming an independent consultant.

With easy-to-read text, *Mind Your Own Business!* is a quick introduction to the information you need to start your own business for an entrepreneurial career.

Chapter 1
Entrepreneurship as a Career

Nearly one million individuals start their own businesses every year.[1] Women have discovered the opportunities that self-employment offers and are starting new businesses at twice the rate of men.[2] Self-employment is an important career option that needs to be considered by talented individuals experienced in business operations. This book helps you answer the important question, "Should I go into business for myself?" Whether the answer is yes, no, or maybe, you will be better prepared to make an important career decision.

Small Business as a Viable Career

As you consider whether to become an entrepreneur, it is useful to define what a small business is. The task is not easy, though, because small businesses vary considerably in size. For example, the federal government has specific definitions for different types of industries. A manufacturing business that has as many as 500 employees is nevertheless considered a small business as long as it does not dominate its industry. Some guidelines define small retail businesses through dollar volume, which typically ranges from $2 million to $7 million. However, 88.9% of all businesses in the United States have fewer than 10 employees.[3] Your local Small Business Administration (SBA) office can provide information on the typical size of a small business in your field of interest.

Small businesses generate jobs, are highly creative, and support major business efforts. To understand the importance of small businesses to the economy, consider the following statistics that come from a variety of sources on small business management:

- 700,000 to 1,300,000 new businesses are started each year in the U.S.[4]

- Between 13 million and 19 million small businesses exist in the U.S.[5]

- Small businesses generate 37% of the Gross National Product.[6]

- Small businesses created 80% of all new jobs in the 1970s and 1980s and will probably provide more than 60% for the 1990s.[7]

- Small businesses provide 65% of all workers with their first job.[8]

- Small businesses account for 50% of all inventions and 95% of all radical inventions (such as copiers, instant photographs, personal computers, etc.) since World War II.[9]

- Small businesses produce 24 times more inventions for research dollars spent than do large businesses.[10]

Why do people decide to start their own business? The answer is not a simple one. For some, starting a business is an exciting prospect they have often dreamed about. Launching a business enables them to fulfill this dream of becoming part of the dynamic arena of small business. Sometimes a person doesn't start a business intentionally but rather as a result of a unique set of circumstances. A person seldom has only one reason for starting a business; usually several motivational forces are at work. Here are some of the common reasons for starting a business.

Independence
Many people become self-employed because they believe self-employment will offer them independence and control over their own work. To a certain extent this is true. You will be able to determine what goals you want to accomplish, what projects you want to conduct, how your business will be run, who will be hired, and how much you will earn. However, your independence is limited when you have to satisfy the needs and demands of customers, provide regular paychecks to employees, pay vendors in a timely manner, and meet government regulations. But these constraints affect all businesses. As a self-em-

ployed individual, you can nevertheless make the decisions about how all of these constraints will affect the operation of your business.

Job satisfaction

Entrepreneurs gain a great deal of satisfaction from their jobs. They know that they are responsible for their own success and failure. They know also that they will not be denied the recognition and credit they deserve.

Financial achievement

Most people become self-employed for financial gain. Even those who start a nonprofit organization expect to receive a reasonable salary from the enterprise. An entrepreneur usually establishes three goals for financial success. The first is to earn as much money through self-employment as one would earn working for someone else. The second is to create a new business to increase earning potential. The third is to have the potential to make more money than one would expect to earn through traditional work opportunities. The original motivation for establishing a business may change throughout the entrepreneur's career.

Career opportunity

Some people start their own business because they find it a desirable career opportunity. In today's society, entrepreneurship is viewed as a high-status career. People such as Steve Jobs (cofounder of Apple Computer), Bill Gates (creator of Microsoft), Thomas Monaghan (founder of Domino's Pizza), and Fred Smith (founder of Federal Express) have continued to perpetuate the image of the entrepreneur as a hero in American business.

Myths about Small Business

A realistic assessment of your interest in self-employment requires that you examine four common myths about entrepreneurship. In this section each myth is explained, and you are asked to develop conclusions about the impact each might have on the business you start.

Myth #1:

Entrepreneurs are born, not made.

Some people feel that they just aren't made to be entrepreneurs. They seem to believe that successful entrepreneurs are born with a certain set of characteristics. However, research has identified more than 40 characteristics of successful entrepreneurs.[11] Not all entrepreneurs possess these characteristics. Furthermore, the study of entrepreneurship has shown that experience and knowledge are far more critical to success than are personal characteristics. Your business knowledge and experience will contribute to your mastery of self-employment.

You can increase your ability to have a successful small business by learning as much as you can about starting and managing small businesses. List resources you could use to improve your entrepreneurial knowledge and skills.

1. _____

2. _____

3. _____

4. _____

5. _____

6. _____

7. _____

8. _____

You needn't worry if your list is short. More resources are listed later in this chapter in a section titled "Help for Small Business Development."

Myth #2:

The rate of small business failures is extremely high.

Most people have read statistics that indicate a high rate of failure among new enterprises. Rates as high as 80% of businesses failing within the first five years have been reported. Surprisingly, many businesses that close are not in financial trouble but are terminated for other reasons.

Some people shut down their business because they want to spend more time with their family, they want to sell the business for a profit, they go into another new enterprise, or they choose to close before they experience any financial loss. The most recent statistics from the Department of Commerce indicate that fewer than 1% of all businesses were forced into bankruptcy during the period of 1972-86. The number of new businesses that close within a five-year period may approach 50%, but the reasons for closure are not necessarily due to financial failures. The financial risk involved in starting a new business is therefore not as great as might be expected.

Why do small businesses fail, then? Some people report that while they were prepared to deliver a product or service, they did not have the necessary expertise in finance and management. Others were not prepared for how vulnerable a small business can be when a bad decision is made or a contract falls through.

Most people know of new businesses that start in a community and then fail. List some of the reasons you think these businesses have failed.

1. _____

2. _____

3. _____

4. _____

5. _____

6. _____

7. _____

8. _____

Myth #3:
You need money to start your own business.

Adequate financing is important for your new business. One of the major reasons that new businesses fail is poor financial planning for business needs. However, the new entrepreneur can use many strategies to identify financial resources and control costs. Financial resources may be obtained from personal investments and savings, loans from banks or friends, or guaranteed work from a customer. Costs can be controlled by starting the business at home, sharing an office with someone else, using a secretarial service, or buying used equipment. You need to identify available financial resources for starting a business and then compare these with estimated costs.

List your resources for working capital for a new business and the innovative cost-control methods you might use.

Financial Resources	**Cost-Control Methods**
_____	_____
_____	_____
_____	_____
_____	_____
_____	_____
_____	_____

Myth #4:
Most small businesses fail because of uncontrollable factors.

A survey conducted by Minolta and reported in USA Today identified five major reasons for small business failure. (Note: Because respondents could choose more than one answer, the percentage reported is greater than 100%.) Nearly 50% of small business owners identified a lack of capital as the primary reason for failure. Twenty-three percent said that failure was brought about through no business knowledge, and another 19% indicated that failure was due to poor management. The final two reasons given were inadequate planning (15%) and inexperience (15%).[12] All of these factors, however, are ones you can control. To avoid potential problems that might affect your business, you must do adequate planning. A successful enterprise is the result of careful preparation and hard work rather than luck.

Describe the strategies you would use to avoid the problems identified in the survey as contributing to business failures.

1. _____

_____

2. _____

_____

3. _____

_____

4. _____

_____

5. _____

_____

Why Self-Employment Is Easier Today

In many ways becoming self-employed today is easier than it has been in the past. This should be encouraging to those who are thinking about becoming self-employed. In this section several reasons are given for this positive environment for self-employment, including resources that can help you start your business.

Capitalization
A number of sources currently exist for venture capital. Additionally, the home equity loan makes it possible for some individuals to invest in a small business opportunity.

Lump-sum distributions

With a number of companies offering early retirement or the opportunity to sever employment, many individuals are given a severance package or pension benefit as a lump-sum distribution. This provides capital to invest in a business venture.

Computers and other electronic devices

Computers and other electronic devices, such as laser printers and fax machines, make it easier for someone to prepare proposals, write business plans, and compare financial options. With a computer and modem, a person can access remote databases for information important to a small business and can complete tasks without hiring a consultant.

Franchises

With the growing popularity of franchises, individuals can buy into an existing business without developing an original service or product. Some people prefer working with a tested idea instead of starting a business of their own.

State-wide programs for small business development

A number of state and national programs are designed to help small businesses. Some of these programs are described in the next section.

Help for Small Business Development

The current business climate supports small business development. Many states have special programs to encourage small businesses. Those who make use of such resources will have a better chance of success in an adverse economy than those who do not. Check with your state to see what programs are available in your geographic location.

Training and retraining programs

These programs are designed to train workers, retrain displaced workers, provide literacy and basic education to the work force, and educate individuals on what it takes to become self-employed.

Incubator programs

Incubator programs are called by many names, depending on the locale. They may be called centers for technology, innovation, or enterprise.

The program usually involves multitenant buildings that cater to small businesses or new business start-ups. Rent is usually below market price. Often included in the rent are a variety of office services, such as secretarial support, janitorial services, and rooms for meetings and conferences. Additional services might include financial services, marketing support, and technical assistance. The advantages of an incubator program are affordable rent, a variety of useful services, and a supportive environment.

Small Business Administration Minority Assistance
The Small Business Administration has special programs for members of minority groups. These programs provide management and technical assistance for targeted groups. The Small Business Administration joins forces with private industry, banks, local communities, and governmental agencies to provide resources for individuals with special social and economic needs. The Department of Commerce also provides assistance through a network of local business development organizations.

Small Business Development Center (SBDC)
The Small Business Development Center is a cooperative venture between the Small Business Administration and local businesses. It is designed to provide counseling and information to potential small business owners.

Small Business Loan program
Loan programs are available through the Small Business Administration to make financing available to persons who cannot obtain financing in the private credit marketplace. Numerous programs are designed to help various segments of the small business community finance effective business plans.

Small Business Innovation Research (SBIR) program
The small business research programs have four goals: to stimulate technological innovation; to use small business to meet federal research and development. Programs draw on the resources of federal departments and agencies, such as The Department of Defense, Health and Human Services, and Department of Energy.

Service Corps of Retired Executives (SCORE) &
Active Corps of Executives (ACE)

These two programs are sponsored by the SBA and consist of volunteers who provide free consulting services. By using these programs, you can build on the practical experience of executives who have dealt with many of the problems you are likely to encounter in your own business.

Federal Farmers Home Administration

Loan programs are available through the Federal Farmers Home Administration and are intended to promote economic development of small businesses in rural areas.

Economic Development Administration (EDA)

The Economic Development Administration offers loan guarantees for the financing of projects that will help create or retain private sector employment in targeted areas and to facilitate industrial and economic growth. The EDA was created to generate jobs and to stimulate commercial and industrial growth in economically distressed areas.

All of the preceding programs are free services and resources that can be used by an entrepreneur to learn more about how to engage in successful self-employment opportunities.

Summary

This chapter examined the impact of small business on the U.S. economy. You learned why entrepreneurship can be a viable career. You were given a review of myths about self-employment plus an explanation of why they are not true. The chapter further examined why self-employment is easier today and provided a survey of government programs available to assist the entrepreneur.

Endnotes

1. Leon C. Megginson, Charles R. Scott, and William L. Megginson, *Successful Small Business Management* (Homewood, IL: Irwin, 1991), p. 5.

2. "Different Motivation for Women Owners," *The Wall Street Journal,* July 7, 1989, p. B1.

3. "Enterprise Statistics," U.S. Department of Commerce (Washington, D.C.: U.S. Government Printing Office, 1982), Table 3.

4. Jeffry A. Timmons, *New Venture Creation: Entrepreneurship in the 1990s* (Homewood, IL: Irwin, 1990), p. 4.

5. U.S. Small Business Administration, reported by the National Institute of Business Management, Inc., *Research Recommendations,* April 10, 1989, p. 2.

6. Ralph M. Gaedeke and Dennis H. Tootelian, *Small Business Management,* 3rd ed. (Boston: Allyn and Bacon, 1991), p. 9.

7. *The State of Small Business: A Report of the President* (Washington, D.C.: U.S. Government Printing Office, 1988), p. 51.

8. Charles R. Kuehl and Peggy A. Lambing, *Small Business: Planning and Management* (Chicago: The Dryden Press, 1990), p. 6.

9. Timmons, p. 4.

10. U.S. Congress, Senate, Joint Hearings before the Select Committee on Small Business and Other Committees, *Small Business and Innovation,* August 9-10, 1978, p. 7.

11. John A. Hornaday, "Research about Living Entrepreneurs," *Encyclopedia of Entrepreneurship,* ed. Kent, Sexton & Vesper (Englewood Cliffs, NJ: Prentice Hall, Inc., 1982), pp. 26-27.

12. *USA Today,* March 13, 1987, p. 13.

Chapter 2
Assessing Your
Entrepreneurial Abilities

The main objective of this chapter is to help you determine whether you have the potential to be an entrepreneur. To achieve this objective, the chapter first describes the characteristics and skills of successful entrepreneurs so that you can realistically appraise entrepreneurship as a career. The chapter then helps you assess your own characteristics and skills in order to see whether you have similar strengths for an entrepreneurial career.

Entrepreneurial Career Assessment

The *Entrepreneurial Career Assessment Form* is designed to introduce you to many of the characteristics of successful entrepreneurs. This self-evaluation can provide you with some guidance about the appropriateness of an entrepreneurial career for you. For the evaluation to be effective, you should respond to the questions in an honest and accurate manner.

Read the statements carefully, interpreting each one in the context of your personal experience. Determine how strongly you agree or disagree with the accuracy of the statement in describing yourself. Use the following scale to indicate your responses. Write the most appropriate number in the box before each statement.

Entrepreneurial Career Assessment Form

Strongly Agree		Somewhat Agree		Strongly Disagree
5	4	3	2	1

_____ 1. I am willing to work 50 hours or more per week regularly.

_____ 2. My family will support my going into business.

_____ 3. I am willing to accept both financial and career risks when necessary.

_____ 4. I don't need all the fringe benefits provided by conventional employment.

_____ 5. I would like to take full responsibility for the successes and failures of my business.

_____ 6. I would experience more financial success by operating my own business.

_____ 7. I feel a great deal of pride when I complete a project successfully.

_____ 8. I have a high energy level that can be maintained over a long time.

_____ 9. I enjoy controlling my own work assignments and making all decisions that affect my work.

_____ 10. I believe that I am primarily responsible for my own successes and failures.

_____ 11. I have a strong desire to achieve positive results even when it requires a great deal of additional effort.

_____ 12. I have a good understanding of how to manage a business.

_____ 13. I can function in ambiguous situations.

_____ 14. One or both of my parents were entrepreneurs.

_____ 15. I believe that my abilities and skills are greater than those of most of my coworkers.

_____ 16. People trust me and consider me honest and reliable.

_____ 17. I always try to complete every project I start, regardless of obstacles and difficulties.

_____ 18. I am willing to do something even when other people laugh or belittle me for doing it.

_____ 19. I can make decisions quickly.

_____ 20. I have a good network of friends, professionals, and business acquaintances.

_____ **TOTAL**

Total the numbers you placed before the statements and enter the total in the space provided. Then refer to the following chart to determine a general assessment of your suitability for self-employment.

Score   **Assessment**

80 - 100 You have outstanding ability to be an entrepreneur.

60 - 79 You have satisfactory ability to be an entrepreneur.

40 - 59 Self-employment may not be an appropriate career for you.

0 - 39 Probably you should avoid an entrepreneur career.

Characteristics of an Entrepreneur

The following list describes some common characteristics of an entrepreneur. The number(s) after each characteristic indicates the related statement(s) in the assessment form. This list interprets the form qualitatively. Note that arriving at a conclusive portrait of a typical entrepreneur is very difficult. Therefore, you may score low on the assessment and still succeed as an entrepreneur.

Works hard (Statements 1 and 8)
Self-employment requires a great deal of time and effort. The entrepreneur must perform a wide variety of time-consuming tasks. Seventy-seven percent of all entrepreneurs report working 50 or more hours per week, and 54% say that they work more than 60 hours per week.[1] Such a time commitment requires that you have a high energy level.

Has family support (Statement 2)

A successful entrepreneur needs family support.[2] If you are married, your spouse must believe in your business because it will require that both of you sacrifice time and money. The stress may create disruptions in family relationships. If you have children, they will need encouragement in understanding your need to spend so much time away from the family. The more positive support you receive from your family, the more you can concentrate on making the business a success.

Takes risks (Statement 3)

Entrepreneurs are risk takers.[3] They risk their careers, time, and money in order to make a success of their businesses. A review of the research on this subject finds that most entrepreneurs perceive risks differently than other people. What others see as a risk, the entrepreneur sees as a controllable situation. Entrepreneurs will try to organize a risky situation by identifying resources, ordering them for a purpose, and scheduling their use appropriately. To be successful in self-employment, you should feel comfortable taking reasonable risks.

Sacrifices employment benefits (Statement 4)

One of the major realities of self-employment is that you won't receive a regular paycheck. You pay for your own fringe benefits. A nice office, secretarial assistance, equipment, and other features of employment you have grown to expect are no longer available unless you provide them for yourself.

Is independent (Statements 5 and 9)

Entrepreneurs like being independent and in control of situations.[4] Many people who become self-employed consider the opportunity to be their own boss as one of the major benefits of self-employment. Although being independent may not be a major concern for you, it is certainly an aspect of self-employment that you need to feel comfortable with. If you cannot afford to hire other employees when you begin your business, you may at first be lonely as a self-employed person.

Wants financial success (Statement 6)

A primary reason that most entrepreneurs have for going into business is to achieve financial success.[5] The desire for financial success provides motivational drive for the self-employed person. If you want to be an entrepreneur, you need to establish a reasonable financial goal that you want to achieve through self-employment. This goal will help you measure how well you are doing in fulfilling your personal needs through an entrepreneurial career.

Is energetic (Statements 1 and 8)

Self-employment requires long work hours. You will frequently be unable to control the number of hours required to fulfill all the necessary tasks. The entrepreneur must have a high energy level to respond to the job's demands. In fact, an entrepreneur will often be energized by the work that is demanded and finds an energy loss when "relaxing." You will need stamina that allows you to work 12- to 16-hour days, 6- to 7-day weeks, and 52-week years.

Has an internal "locus of control" (Statement 10)

Successful entrepreneurs have an internal *locus of control,* or inner sense of responsibility for the outcome of a venture.[6] Research evidence shows that an internal locus of control increases creativity and activity. To be an entrepreneur, you should have a strong sense of being a "victor" who is responsible for your actions. If, however, you frequently consider yourself a "victim" and blame other people, bad luck, or difficult circumstances for your failures, entrepreneurship might not be the right career move for you.

Has a need to achieve (Statements 7 and 11)

Entrepreneurs have a strong need for achievement.[7] They strive to excel and accomplish objectives that are quite high. If you want to become an entrepreneur, you should be willing to set high goals for yourself and enjoy striving to achieve those goals.

Has business experience (Statement 12)

An entrepreneur should have extensive business experience to be successful.[8] General management experience is beneficial because an entrepreneur should know something about all types of management. Formal training and education in management also are helpful. Your knowledge and experience will be more formally assessed in the next exercise in this chapter.

Has a self-employed parent as a role model (Statement 14)

Research has shown that entrepreneurs are more likely to have a parent—especially a father—who is self-employed.[9] A parent's inspiration and knowledge about operating a business can contribute to an entrepreneur's success. If you have a parent who is self-employed, consider this a plus for your own success as an entrepreneur.

Has self-confidence (Statements 10, 15, and 18)

An important characteristic of entrepreneurs is self-confidence.[10] This factor is particularly important when you face major challenges and difficulties with your business. You need to believe in yourself. Your belief will help you overcome the problems that inevitably affect all self-employed persons at some point in their careers.

Has integrity (Statement 16)

People often cite honesty and integrity as characteristics of entrepreneurs.[11] Customers do not want to deal with business owners who are dishonest and unethical. You should feel positive about your ethical treatment of people and be committed to conducting your business with the utmost integrity.

Has determination (Statement 17)

One of the most important characteristics of entrepreneurs is determination.[12] This trait is closely related to self-confidence. The more you believe in yourself, the more likely you are to continue to struggle for success when faced with tremendous obstacles. You need determination in order to overcome the problems that beset every new venture.

Adapts to change (Statements 13 and 19)

A new business changes rapidly, so an entrepreneur must be able to adapt to change.[13] Two primary skills are required for adaptation to change: the capacity to solve problems, and the ability to make quick decisions. Another skill is the ability to learn from your experiences and to seek formal learning that will help solve your problems. To be a successful entrepreneur, you will need all of these capabilities.

Has a good network of professionals (Statement 20)

An entrepreneur has a good network of professionals.[14] This network provides access to those who can be consulted for advice, information, and referrals. You should have an extensive network of professionals to whom you can turn for assistance

Now return to the *Entrepreneurial Career Assessment Form* and identify the three entrepreneurial characteristics you feel are your strongest.

1. _____

2. _____

3. _____

Assessing Your Marketable Skills

To be an entrepreneur, you should not only possess some of the characteristics common to successful entrepreneurs but also have the skills needed for successful self-employment. This section helps you assess those skills.

Identifying Your Areas of Proficiency

As you consider self-employment, you should determine your most marketable skills. Although you probably don't possess every skill in the following lists, you have undoubtedly gained some degree of proficiency in a number of them. For each skill, circle the number that best approximates your degree of proficiency.

	Degree of Proficiency					
Communication Skills	**No Skill**					**Mastery**
Corresponding	0	1	2	3	4	5
Editing	0	1	2	3	4	5
Writing	0	1	2	3	4	5
Drawing	0	1	2	3	4	5
Interviewing	0	1	2	3	4	5
Listening	0	1	2	3	4	5
Relating to customers	0	1	2	3	4	5
Presenting ideas	0	1	2	3	4	5
Public speaking	0	1	2	3	4	5
Facilitating	0	1	2	3	4	5
Managing conflicts	0	1	2	3	4	5
Mediating	0	1	2	3	4	5
Negotiating	0	1	2	3	4	5

Human Resource Skills	Degree of Proficiency					
	No Skill					Mastery
Coaching	0	1	2	3	4	5
Counseling	0	1	2	3	4	5
Teaching	0	1	2	3	4	5
Developing others	0	1	2	3	4	5
Helping others	0	1	2	3	4	5
Motivating	0	1	2	3	4	5
Team building	0	1	2	3	4	5
Training	0	1	2	3	4	5
Assessing performance	0	1	2	3	4	5
Coordinating Skills						
Scheduling	0	1	2	3	4	5
Following up	0	1	2	3	4	5
Reporting	0	1	2	3	4	5
Recording	0	1	2	3	4	5
Cataloging	0	1	2	3	4	5
Correcting	0	1	2	3	4	5
Data Management Skills						
Assessing quality	0	1	2	3	4	5
Using a computer	0	1	2	3	4	5
Measuring	0	1	2	3	4	5
Setting standards	0	1	2	3	4	5
Taking inventory	0	1	2	3	4	5
Managing information	0	1	2	3	4	5
Gathering data	0	1	2	3	4	5
General Management Skills						
Advising	0	1	2	3	4	5
Approving	0	1	2	3	4	5
Making decisions	0	1	2	3	4	5
Developing procedures	0	1	2	3	4	5
Developing systems	0	1	2	3	4	5
Directing	0	1	2	3	4	5
Delegating	0	1	2	3	4	5
Implementing	0	1	2	3	4	5
Instructing	0	1	2	3	4	5

	Degree of Proficiency					
General Management Skills	**No Skill**					**Mastery**
Interpreting policy	0	1	2	3	4	5
Managing details	0	1	2	3	4	5
Managing people	0	1	2	3	4	5
Managing tasks	0	1	2	3	4	5
Problem solving	0	1	2	3	4	5
Project managing	0	1	2	3	4	5
Serving as change agent	0	1	2	3	4	5
Financial Management Skills						
Analyzing budgets	0	1	2	3	4	5
Analyzing finances	0	1	2	3	4	5
Researching and analyzing economics	0	1	2	3	4	5
Auditing	0	1	2	3	4	5
Budgeting	0	1	2	3	4	5
Cost accounting	0	1	2	3	4	5
Managing finances	0	1	2	3	4	5
Financial planning	0	1	2	3	4	5
Fund-raising	0	1	2	3	4	5
Planning Skills						
Analyzing	0	1	2	3	4	5
Conceptualizing	0	1	2	3	4	5
Desiging	0	1	2	3	4	5
Developing strategies	0	1	2	3	4	5
Developing policies and procedures	0	1	2	3	4	5
Researching	0	1	2	3	4	5
Reviewing	0	1	2	3	4	5
Surveying	0	1	2	3	4	5
Sales and Marketing Skills						
Selling	0	1	2	3	4	5
Marketing	0	1	2	3	4	5
Writing proposals	0	1	2	3	4	5
Pricing	0	1	2	3	4	5
Analyzing markets	0	1	2	3	4	5

	Degree of Proficiency					
Sales and Marketing Skills	**No Skill**				**Mastery**	
Forecasting	0	1	2	3	4	5
Advertising	0	1	2	3	4	5
Promoting	0	1	2	3	4	5
Managing sales	0	1	2	3	4	5
Relating to clients	0	1	2	3	4	5
Customer Service Skills						
Serving customers	0	1	2	3	4	5
Responding promptly	0	1	2	3	4	5
Building relations	0	1	2	3	4	5
Handling complaints	0	1	2	3	4	5
Technical Skills						
Engineering	0	1	2	3	4	5
Programming	0	1	2	3	4	5
Tooling	0	1	2	3	4	5
Inventing	0	1	2	3	4	5
Manufacturing	0	1	2	3	4	5
Designing	0	1	2	3	4	5
Developing products	0	1	2	3	4	5
Organizational Skills						
Administering	0	1	2	3	4	5
Categorizing	0	1	2	3	4	5
Developing work plans	0	1	2	3	4	5
Setting priorities	0	1	2	3	4	5
Assigning	0	1	2	3	4	5
Clarifying vision and mission	0	1	2	3	4	5

Specialized Skills

Specify the technical skills that you have developed and indicate your degree of proficiency.

Degree of Proficiency

No Skill				Mastery	

0	1	2	3	4	5
0	1	2	3	4	5
0	1	2	3	4	5
0	1	2	3	4	5
0	1	2	3	4	5

Identifying Your Strongest Skills

Go back through the lists of skills and identify those you rated the highest. Write these skills on a piece of paper and then rank them from the strongest to weakest. Write the top six skills in the following spaces.

1. _____

2. _____

3. _____

4. _____

5. _____

6. _____

Identifying Your Most Important Skills for Success

Which three highest-rated skills stand out as ones that would help you succeed in self-employment? Write these skills in the following spaces.

1. _____

2. _____

3. _____

The Pros and Cons of Self-Employment

Now that you've completed the assessment exercises in this chapter, assess the positive and negative aspects of self-employment for yourself. On the positive side, list the characteristics and skills that you feel will help you succeed as an entrepreneur. On the negative side, list the characteristics and skills that you lack and will thus need to overcome in order to be a successful entrepreneur.

Positives	Negatives

Write a short paragraph explaining whether you believe that self-employment is a good career option. State clearly the reasons for your conclusion about the appropriateness of self-employment for you. Share this summary with three people who know you well and ask them for an evaluation of your conclusion.

_____

_____

_____

_____

_____

_____

_____

_____

_____

_____

_____

_____

_____

_____

_____

_____

_____

Summary

This chapter provided a series of exercises to help you evaluate yourself as a potential candidate for entrepreneurial self-employment. A self-evaluation form helped you assess your suitability for self-employment. You learned about some common characteristics of entrepreneurs to help you determine whether you too shared some of these characteristics. You also identified your skills to arrive at a sense of your strongest skills and particularly those that might be most important for success. In view of your skills, you weighed the pros and cons of self-employment and expressed in a prose statement your conclusion about the suitability of self-employment for you. Such a conclusion is a necessary first step in thinking about starting your own business.

Endnotes

1. Mark Robichaux, "Business First, Family Second," *The Wall Street Journal,* May 12, 1989, p. B1.

2. Charles R. Kuehl and Peggy A. Lambing, *Small Business: Planning and Management* (Chicago: Dryden Press, 1990), pp. 41-42.

3. Nicholas C. Siropolis, *Small Business Management: A Guide to Entrepreneurship* (Boston: Houghton Mifflin Company, 1990), p. 45.

4. Donald F. Kuratko and Richard M. Hodgetts, *Entrepreneurship: A Contemporary Approach* (Chicago: Dryden Press, 1989), p. 73.

5. Ralph M. Gaedeke and Dennis H. Tootelian, *Small Business Management,* 3rd ed. (Boston: Allyn and Bacon, 1991), p. 73.

6. Barbara J. Bird, *Entrepreneurial Behavior* (Glenview, IL: Scott Foresman and Company, 1989), p. 82.

7. David C. McClelland, *The Achieving Society* (New York: Van Nostrand, 1961).

8. Karl H. Vesper, *New Venture Strategies* (Englewood Cliffs, NJ: Prentice Hall, Inc., 1990), p. 39.

9. Robert D. Hisrich and Michael P. Peters, *Entrepreneurship: Starting, Developing, and Managing a New Enterprise* (Homewood, IL: BPI Irwin, 1989), pp. 55-57.

10. Siropolis, p. 45.

11. John A. Hornaday, "Research about Living Entrepreneurs," *Encyclopedia of Entrepreneurship,* ed. Kent, Sexton & Vesper (Englewood Cliffs, NJ: Prentice Hall, Inc., 1982), pp. 26-27.

12. Jeffry A. Timmons, *New Venture Creation: Entrepreneurship in the 1990s* (Homewood, IL: Irwin, 1990), pp. 165-167.

13. Gaedeke and Tootelian, pp. 88-89.

14. Hisrich and Peters, p. 64.

Chapter 3
Starting a Business

In chapter 2, you examined the characteristics of an entrepreneur and determined how many of them you possess. Now you examine what type of self-employment is most appropriate for you.

People often think of an entrepreneur as someone who has a new idea for a product or service and then creates a business to sell that new product or service. But being an entrepreneur doesn't always mean being creative.

To become self-employed, you can choose one of three options. One option—the obvious one—is to start a new business based on your own idea. A second option is to purchase an existing business from someone else. And a third is to buy a franchise, which is typically a program that assists you in duplicating a successful business created by someone else. This chapter helps you understand the benefits of each approach to business creation and determine which option is the most appropriate for you.

Starting Your Own Business

You might consider starting your own business if you have a product or service in mind that interests you. Some individuals want to start a business because they have been in a field for some time and have an idea of how things could be done better.

Perhaps a person is in sales and has consistently heard her customers request a certain product or suggest product improvements. Possibly she has been thinking about the perfect design for years and is now ready to design the ideal product.

Another individual may have been serving customers for a long time in a customer-driven industry, such as travel or mail services. This individual may have been critical of his employer's lack of creativity and flexibility in meeting customer needs. He is convinced that he can provide a better service at a reduced cost by keeping overhead down and customer service up.

After working at a hobby for years, still another individual might decide that it is time to give up the steady paycheck and to spend full time with the hobby. This person has become an expert with the hobby and now wants to make a profit through that expertise.

Advantages of Starting Your Own Business

Starting a business has many advantages, especially these:

- Starting your own business gives you more freedom in what you do and how you do it.

- Launching a new business avoids inheriting problems from a previous owner or facing restrictions from a franchisor.

- Starting your own business can usually be done with a smaller amount of capital.

- Owning the business you start and watching it grow can be very satisfying.

- Basing your own business on a new idea and a well-thought-out plan can be quite profitable.

Disadvantages of Starting
Your Own Business

Starting a business has also a number of disadvantages. These include the following:

- It generally takes more time for a new business to become profitable.
- During the early stages of a new business, you may need to invest a great amount of time and money in research, marketing, and financing your business.
- A new business based on an innovative product or service may need additional capital during the start-up period to cover the time required to educate potential buyers about the new product or service.
- Starting a new business requires a number of business skills, such as time management, marketing, budgeting, and goal setting. Some specific technical skills may be required also.

Origins of
a New Business

A new business idea usually originates in one of three ways: opportunity recognition, idea generation, or serendipity.[1] This section describes each of these possible origins.

Recognition of an opportunity

One way to create a business is to spot an opportunity. For example, several enterprising people recognized that the Gulf War provided an opportunity for producing T-shirts with a wide range of themes related to the war. This opportunity was short-lived because the war did not last long, but other opportunities can be long term. An example of a long-term opportunity is the business of recharging toner cartridges for copiers and laser printers—an opportunity that has resulted from the growing use of copy machines and personal computers in business. Another example is the business of providing quick oil changes for people who don't have the time or the ability to change the oil themselves and don't want to be inconvenienced by long waits at other car maintenance shops.

Sometimes an opportunity arises when you recognize a way to apply an old idea to a new situation. For example, Famous Amos cookies took the traditional Toll House cookie and changed it so that it appealed to a different segment of the population.

To recognize opportunities, you need to be a good observer of the economy, business activities, and social developments. Entrepreneurs who were tracking the increased emphasis on health recognized the potential for frozen yogurt as a low-fat substitute for ice cream. You can track economic, business, and social trends by reading business periodicals and general-interest magazines, talking with people about trends, analyzing developing trends, and thinking about products or services that will be bought by people because of these trends.

An important factor in looking for opportunities is timing. Trying to market an excellent product or service before consumers are ready to purchase it will result in limited success or failure.

List specific ways you could watch for trends that offer business opportunities.

1. _____

2. _____

3. _____

4. _____

5. _____

Describe the methods you would use to analyze the feasibility of a new business opportunity resulting from economic, business, or social trends.

1. _____

   _____

2. _____

   _____

3. _____

   _____

4. _____

   _____

5. _____

   _____

6. _____

   _____

A new idea

The creation of a new product or service that no one has previously marketed is called *idea generation*. Personal computers, compact discs, video cameras, and video games are examples of products for which a market didn't exist before 1975. Personal computers and video games were created by people with a new idea who started small companies with very little money. Today huge companies sell these products to billion-dollar markets. Service businesses, which were virtually nonexistent 15 years ago, provide video rentals, 24-hour medical care, 1-hour photo processing, mail services, and child care for sick children.

Do you have an idea for a new product or service that you believe could become a successful business? Describe the idea in the space provided.

_____

_____

_____

_____

_____

_____

What are some of the obstacles you would face in developing this idea into a business?

1. _____

2. _____

3. _____

4. _____

5. _____

6. _____

How could each of these obstacles be overcome?

1. _____

2. _____

3. _____

4. _____

5. _____

6. _____

Serendipity

A business that originates from serendipity is largely unplanned. In popular terms it is called "being in the right place at the right time." However, serendipity often occurs because an individual is looking for ways to start a business and recognizes how a situation could lead to such an opportunity. For example, you might be approached by a former employer who doesn't want to hire you but will give you a consulting contract. This could lead to your starting a full-time consulting business. Another possibility is that you meet a manufacturer who is having difficulty finding a supplier of a particular component. You happen to know of a source for the component. The manufacturer then offers you the opportunity to become the supplier. From this one account, you are able to start a business and obtain other accounts.

Sometimes serendipity is called luck. Many successful people, however, insist that you make your own luck. You increase the chance for this type of serendipitous occurrence by contacting people and discussing their needs. Networking is a key skill to practice in seeking serendipitous opportunities.

What skills or specialized knowledge do you possess that could help you take advantage of a serendipitous opportunity? List this information in the space provided.

1. _____

2. _____

3. _____

4. _____

5. _____

6. _____

List also those people whom you could contact to discuss potential business opportunities.

1. _____

2. _____

3. _____

4. _____

5. _____

6. _____

Self-Assessment for Starting a New Business

It is important for you to determine whether starting a new business is your best option in becoming self-employed. Answer the following questions with a T(rue) or F(alse).

_____ I enjoy a high degree of risk in business ventures.

_____ I take great pride in making my personal ideas become reality.

_____ I am willing to invest a great deal of time and money in an untried idea.

_____ I like to establish my own management systems and procedures.

_____ I have or can locate the necessary capital to finance a start-up business.

If you answered True to four or more of these questions, including the last one, you would be a good prospect for creating a new business.

Buying a Business

You might consider buying an existing business if you want to be a business owner but don't want to go through the pains of starting your own business. Some individuals may be uncertain of how to do this, or they lack (or think they lack) the creativity, talent, or special skills to start their own business.

An individual might want more flexibility and freedom on the job. After being in a corporation for a long time, following the chain of command, and marching to someone else's drum, this person might decide to call the shots, earn more money, and have more say in how things are done.

Perhaps an individual wants to retire but continue working. Such an individual might be interested in buying a business that provides an income but is not as constricting as a full-time job. This person may decide to buy a business and hire someone to run it.

An individual who has owned other businesses and spent much time and money getting them started might want to buy another business. Having learned a great deal about what makes businesses successful, this person might be interested in shopping around for a business that will be profitable from the beginning but will not demand an inordinate amount of time.

Advantages of Buying a Business

Buying a business also has advantages, especially these:

- Purchasing a business usually takes much less time and effort than starting a business.
- An existing business already has a market and customer base.
- Such a business might have a staff and experts in place to work the plan.
- The business has a track record that can be reviewed and evaluated for future profitability.
- If the business is already profitable, it is possible to earn a profit from the beginning.
- If the established business is somewhat successful, the risk is considerably less.
- It is sometimes possible to get a real bargain by buying an existing business.

Disadvantages of Buying a Business

Buying a business likewise has a number of disadvantages, including the following:

- A business for sale may be on the market for internal problems known to the experienced seller but not easily perceived by an inexperienced buyer.
- Even after you have done your homework to find out if an existing business has the right potential, there are no guarantees that the business will continue to be profitable.

- You buy the bad as well as the good about an existing business. It might not be structured the way you would like it to be. The work force might have problems. The business might have a poor location. Accounts receivable might be high and largely uncollectible.

- Most small businesses are successful because of the talent and skills of their owners. You have no way of knowing what effect the owner's departure will have on the business. The owner might be the one most responsible for customer goodwill or have technical knowledge critical to the success of the business.

- The inventory may have book value but may be worthless.

- Buying an existing business might be more expensive than starting one of your own.

Sources for Locating a Business to Purchase

The first step in buying a business is to locate one for sale. You can accomplish this in several ways.

Newspapers and magazines

Advertisements for businesses for sale appear in local papers, *The Wall Street Journal,* and business magazines. These advertisements, however, provide little information for investigating a business and its owners.

Business brokers

Brokers represent companies for sale and usually have extensive information about them. Make certain that the information available from a broker is accurate and verified by an independent source. Remember that a broker represents the interests of the seller. You must therefore exercise a great deal of caution in assessing a deal offered by a broker.

Bankers and accountants

These two groups of professionals work closely with the finances of many small businesses. They are usually in a position to know when owners might be considering a sale but have not yet advertised the business. Working with a banker or an accountant gives you the opportunity to contact a business owner and close a deal without competition from other potential buyers.

Networking

You can contact family members and friends to express an interest in buying a business and ask for their assistance. Be specific about the type of business you are looking for. Contact other professionals you know to discuss your interests and ask for referrals to possible sources. Contact someone who owns the type of business you want to buy and ask whether that individual knows an owner in the industry who may be interested in selling a business.

Evaluating the Business

Evaluating an existing business to determine whether you want to buy it is a critical process. You must devote the time and money needed to do a thorough job. Listed here are some topics that should be included in your evaluation.

Financial records

The owner should pay for an audit that gives an accurate picture of the financial health of the organization. Carefully examine the inventory, equipment, and accounts receivable to determine whether they are up-to-date and worth their book value.

Personnel

A successful business usually has some key employees who are responsible for its success. Talk with these people and determine what their future plans will be. Consider how their plans will affect the business.

Customers

Talk with customers and determine their interest in continuing to do business with the organization once you become the owner. This will help you evaluate how much of an effect the change of ownership will have on goodwill.

Assets

Look at buildings, equipment, furnishings, and inventory to determine their condition. You may need to consult an expert on these matters.

Operations and sales

Observe the business operations. This includes production of goods or services, management systems, and sales. Determine how effective the operations currently are and what expense would be involved in making modifications. Examine the potential growth or decline of sales based on current marketing efforts.

Owner's motivation

Try to discover the owner's real motivation for selling the business. The owner is usually the person who best understands the factors affecting the business. If the owner wants to sell because demand for the product is weakening or insurmountable problems exist with suppliers, you should be cautious. If, however, the owner wants to sell because of illness or a desire to retire, you might be less wary.

Personal preferences

An important aspect in evaluating a business is to determine whether you will personally enjoy operating it. List those items that you feel would be most important to you in purchasing a business.

1. _____

2. _____

3. _____

4. _____

5. _____

6. _____

7. _____

8. _____

9. _____

10. _____

Self-Assessment for Buying a Business

It is important for you to determine whether buying a business is your best option in becoming self-employed. Answer the following questions with a T(rue) or F(alse).

_____ I prefer a low degree of risk in my business ventures.

_____ I like to work with projects that have been started by someone else.

_____ I feel challenged by solving problems that have been created by another person.

_____ I like to delegate some management responsibilities to other people.

_____ I have or can locate the capital necessary to buy an existing business.

If you answered True to four or more of these questions, including the last question, you would be a good prospect for buying a new business.

Buying a Franchise

To become self-employed, you might consider buying a *franchise*. A *franchise* is a product or idea that can be purchased from another person or company along with the expertise to start and operate the business. The buyer of a *franchise* is called a *franchisee,* and the seller is called a *franchisor.*

Who would benefit from buying a franchise? An individual who wants to own a business but doesn't want to suffer the pain of developing a product or service might be interested in buying a franchise. Another individual who wants to start a business but doesn't know what to do or how to get started might like the options a franchise provides.

Advantages of Buying a Franchise

Buying a franchise has certain advantages as well, especially these:

- A franchise product or service has already been developed and field-tested.

- A franchise often has instant name recognition.

- A franchise can earn a profit earlier than a business you start because the products or services are field-tested and known, and you have other franchise models to follow.

- The franchisor provides assistance in starting the franchise business.

- The franchisor can often assist the franchisee in obtaining financing for the new business.

- The franchisee has standardized systems and support materials that make it easier to conduct daily business.

- The franchisor can often provide support through consultants and trainers.

- Other franchisees can offer advice, feedback on their experience, and practical suggestions.

- A franchise business can get high-volume purchase prices for products and cooperate in national advertising campaigns.

Disadvantages of Buying a Franchise

Buying a franchise has some disadvantages too, including these:

- Remember that you are buying a franchise license, which allows you to use the franchise's name, products, and services. For all of these, you pay an established fee. You are not, however, buying a business that includes a building, employees, clients, and so on.

- Your franchise will have certain stipulations about how you use the name, products, and services. As a business owner, you give up a great deal of control when you operate a franchise.

- Some franchises can be purchased for a low fee, but you can pay several hundred thousand dollars for a franchise with a nationally known name. You also have to maintain the business in accordance with standards set by the franchisor, and this can cost extra money.

- The franchisor might terminate your franchise if you don't abide by standards or might be able to buy back the franchise from you whenever the franchisor wants.

- You are dependent on the success of the franchisor. Some franchisees develop an extremely strong business, but when their franchisor goes out of business, they find it impossible to continue operation.

Sources for Locating a Franchise to Purchase

Many of the same sources that were suggested for locating a business to buy can be used to locate a successful franchise to purchase. These include newspapers, magazines, books, business brokers, bankers, accountants, and networking.

Another excellent way to locate a franchise is to visit other cities and talk with business people about the most successful new franchises that have recently come to their city. These investigations may help you identify a franchise that is working successfully but has not yet come to your area. This gives you an opportunity to get a new franchise at a lower cost and become the sole franchise operator for a specific geographic area.

One excellent source of information about franchises is *Entrepreneur* magazine. Each monthly issue has scores of franchise advertisements. An annual issue of *Entrepreneur* provides summary information about hundreds of franchise opportunities.

Evaluating the Franchise

A franchise offers you a business format to use in marketing the product or service that has been developed by the franchisor. You need to study carefully the product or service as well as the format. You must also examine carefully the support the franchisor will provide and the restrictions that will be placed on you as the franchisee. To assist you in this review before you buy the franchise, federal law requires that the franchisor supply the following two documents:

Franchise agreement

This is the contract between the franchisor and the franchisee. It covers such items as costs, obligations of the franchisor and franchisee, conditions and terms, restrictions, and termination of the franchise.

Disclosure statement

This statement, sometimes referred to as a prospectus or offering circular, provides information on 20 topics required by the Federal Trade Commission. This includes franchisor background and experience, other franchisees, background of officers and key management personnel, fee structure, and current legal actions being taken against the franchisor.

In addition to studying these documents, you should find answers to certain questions in evaluating the franchisor. Here are your areas of concern.

Experience

What level of experience does the franchisor have? The franchisor should currently operate several successful businesses and have a history of several years of success. How successful have other franchisees been? You should visit the home office of the franchisor and visit other franchisees.

Trustworthiness

What level of confidence do you have in the trustworthiness of the franchisor? In a sense, you and the franchisor become partners. You must be able to trust and rely on the franchisor. Talk with several franchisees to determine whether they have been treated fairly and honestly.

Expertise

Does the franchisor's staff appear to possess the expertise needed to help you operate a franchise successfully? The operations staff must know not only how to run the business but also how to train you effectively to operate the business. Management procedures and systems should be of a high caliber.

Exclusivity

How exclusive will your franchise be? It is not reasonable to pay a high franchise fee only to have a competitor from the same franchise chain move into your geographic area and take away your business. You need to have geographic protection. Your franchisor can reasonably expect you to produce a specified volume of business within a certain number of years or award the franchise to another individual.

Conditions

How restrictive are the conditions of the franchise agreement? Most franchisors stipulate the store size, decor, personnel requirements, suppliers, methods of operation, accounting procedures, and so on. Conditions will probably be set on the amount of revenue you must generate to retain your franchise. You need to examine all the restrictions that will be placed on you and determine whether they are reasonable and whether you will feel comfortable abiding by them.

Cost

What will the franchise fee be, and what are other costs associated with operating the business?

1. **Franchise fee**

   This is the money you will pay to have the rights to the franchise, receive training, and obtain all the rights granted in the agreement. This can range from no fee to hundreds of thousands of dollars.

2. **Building and equipment**

   You will have to purchase a building and equipment that meet the standards of the franchisor. The franchisor should be able to give you an accurate estimate for this cost. Equipment is usually purchased from the franchisor and might be quite expensive.

3. **Working capital**

   The franchisor will know the amount of funds needed to operate the business in terms of paying personnel, purchasing inventory and supplies, and meeting overhead expenses. The franchisor will know also how many months you should expect to operate before your revenues will be high enough to pay for these expenses. Many franchisors stipulate a specific amount of working capital that must be available to you.

4. Royalties

You will be required to pay the franchisor an annual royalty based on the dollar volume of sales made by your franchise. The royalty may range from 0 to 15 percent.[2]

5. Cooperative national marketing fee

You might be charged a small percentage of your revenue as a contribution for joint national marketing. A franchisor often matches your contribution with an equal contribution to promote marketing.

The field of business franchises has many competitors, and you should look for the one that provides the best program at the most reasonable cost.

Self-Assessment for Buying a Franchise

It is important for you to determine whether buying a franchise is your best option in becoming self-employed. Answer the following questions with a T(rue) or F(alse).

_____ I prefer a very controlled degree of risk in my business ventures.

_____ I feel comfortable working within restrictions set by other people.

_____ I am willing to limit my creativity in order to have a higher level of security.

_____ I do not mind sharing my success, including my profit, with others who contribute to my success.

_____ I have or can locate the capital necessary to buy a franchise.

If you answered True to four or more of these questions, including the last question, you would be a good prospect for buying a franchise.

Summary

To become self-employed, you have several options. You may start your own business, purchase an existing business, or buy a franchise. To determine which option is most appropriate for you, you need to examine your personal interests, skills, temperament, and financial resources. If you take the time to make this assessment, you can choose the best option and feel comfortable with the arrangement.

Endnotes

1. Charles R. Kuehl and Peggy A. Lambing, *Small Business: Planning and Management,* 2nd ed. (Chicago, Dryden Press, 1990), p. 48.

2. Nicholas C. Siropolis, *Small Business Management: A Guide to Entrepreneurship* (Boston: Houghton Mifflin Company, 1990), p. 143.

Chapter 4
Forming an Organization

When you start a new business, you must determine its legal status. Each state has specific legal requirements you must meet to conduct business in the state. You will need to research what these requirements are for your state. You can get this information from the Secretary of State, a local attorney, or government organizations that consult with small businesses.

Legal Status of an Organization

To do business, an organization must have one of four basic types of legal status: sole proprietorship, partnership, limited partnership, or corporation. (A corporation may be set up as a Subchapter S Corporation.) This section describes each type of legal status.

Sole Proprietorship
A sole proprietorship is the simplest legal status for a business and its taxes. When you start a sole proprietorship, you don't need to create a new entity or shift assets. You merely segregate a portion of your assets and dedicate them for business use. You report your business income on your individual tax return, using a schedule that details business expenses and profit.

Partnership

A common law definition of partnership is an association of two or more persons who combine resources and skills to conduct a business. According to the IRS, a partnership may be a syndicate, group, pool, joint venture, or some other unincorporated organization that carries on a venture, business, or financial operation. For federal income tax purposes, a partnership is not classified as a corporation, trust, or estate. The IRS's definition of a partnership is broader than the common law meaning of a partnership. The intentions of a partnership are joint ownership, mutual contribution of capital and services, shared control of the business, and a sharing of profits and losses. Although a partnership does not require a written agreement, it is strongly recommended since the actions of one partner are legally binding on the other partner(s).

Limited Partnership

Two or more persons can form a limited partnership under state law. They must execute a certificate for a limited partnership and file information about themselves with the Secretary of State or a state agency. A limited partnership usually has one or more *general partners,* who are involved in the daily management and operation of the business, and one or more *limited partners*. A limited partnership is often used to attract investors for a business. Through the agreement of a limited partnership, an investor is usually not liable for the obligations of the limited partnership unless the investor is a general partner or takes part in the control of the business.

Corporation

A corporation is a business entity created under state law. In some instances, a corporation may be created under federal law. The corporation must have associates and a purpose for carrying on business. The corporation issues shares of stock to the partners. This provides the legal arrangement for stipulating how profits are divided. Corporations must follow specific state laws for corporations and file annual reports.

Subchapter S Corporation

A Subchapter S Corporation (commonly called an "S Corporation") is a corporation that files for IRS status as an S Corporation. In this type of corporation, all income is taxed through the shareholders even if the income is not actually distributed to the shareholders. An S Corporation is like a partnership because an individual's profits from the business are reported on the individual's income tax return.

You will need to choose the best legal status for your new business. In making this determination, you should consider the following questions:

1. What is the purpose of your business?
2. What are your personal skills and preferences?
3. What kind of organization will your business be?
4. What taxes will you need to pay?

Purpose of the Organization:Profit-making vs Nonprofit

An organization must have a purpose. You need to know what you want to accomplish with the business you start. This will help you choose the best structure for the organization. You can structure your business as either a profit-making organization or a nonprofit organization.

A state has rules governing profit-making and nonprofit organizations. As a potential entrepreneur, you should investigate these state laws carefully and consider whether you want to profit personally from your business. Although a nonprofit organization may generate more revenue than it spends, the principal parties cannot benefit financially from distributions of net revenue. The principal parties can plow profits back into the corporation, but cannot receive distributions of profit from the business. Your business may have to be a nonprofit organization if you want to apply for federal grants or for funds from foundations.

The IRS groups nonprofit organizations into several classes that determine how the organizations are taxed and whether donations to the organizations are tax deductible. To choose the best structure for your organization, you should compare your state's regulations governing nonprofit organizations with IRS regulations. One basic regulation for a nonprofit organization is that it must be incorporated. It therefore cannot be a proprietorship or partnership.

The following questionnaire should help you determine whether a profit-making or nonprofit organization is better for your needs. Answer each question with a T(rue) or F(alse).

_____ Do you want to ask for donations for your organization?

_____ Do you want to start an organization that will provide services to people who will have difficulty paying for them?

_____ Do you want to compete for government grants?

_____ Do you want to qualify for grants from foundations?

_____ Are you more concerned about providing a service than benefiting financially from the organization?

If you responded yes to three or more of these questions, you should think seriously about creating a nonprofit corporation. If you decide at this stage that a nonprofit corporation is the best type of organization for your entrepreneurial activity, the rest of the chapter will be less applicable to you.

Using Personal Skills and Preferences to Determine Business Structure

Your skills and preferences may influence your selection of a legal structure for your business. You may sense that they are more suitable for one type of legal structure than for another. This section examines the relation of personal skills and preferences to each legal form of doing business.

Sole Proprietorship

To operate a sole proprietorship, a person must have general management skills. You need to feel comfortable in the areas of marketing, sales, accounting, finance, human resource management, customer service, facility management, inventory control, and so on. A sole proprietor must therefore have a broad range of expertise. You can hire people who have the skills you lack. However, you must have the resources to afford this expense and be able to supervise these skilled workers. A person who is independent and derives satisfaction from individual accomplishment will probably prefer a sole proprietorship.

Partnership

A partnership is suitable when you need others with more specialized skills. If you find partners with skills that complement your own skills, you will create a stronger business through a larger pool of capabilities for the management and operation of the business. A partnership is suitable also if you need more capital and find partners who can supply it.

A partnership should be based on trust, respect, and mutual appreciation. If this sounds a little like a marriage, you're right. You will have a personal relationship with your partner that will put you in close contact with each other daily. You must develop a comfortable relationship that is also productive. For a successful relationship, each partner needs to appreciate teamwork more than individuality.

Corporation

A corporation requires someone who works well in a team environment. You and other working members of the corporation will have to function as an effective work team. To be a good team member, you need to respect and trust the other members of the corporation. You will often need to forgo your preferences to promote the overall good of the corporation. Working on a team, however, spreads the risk for the business venture among the owners. Therefore, a corporation might appeal to someone who wants to reduce the risk of going into business.

Self-Assessment for Determining Business Structure

Complete the following questionnaire to assess which form of legal structure best fits your skills and preferences. Check each statement that applies to you.

_____ I enjoy freedom and independence in decision making.

_____ I believe that teamwork is superior to individual pursuits.

_____ I have all the skills needed to operate a business successfully.

_____ I believe that an organization can benefit from the questions and challenges that members pose to one another.

_____ I value a strong relationship with a few people compared to a good relationship with many people.

_____ I like to reduce personal risk by sharing it with other people.

_____ I prefer to optimize my financial gains even if I must do all the work myself.

_____ I believe that it is better to do a job myself than to rely on someone else.

Answer Key

If you checked statements 1, 3, 7, and 8, a **sole proprietorship** may be the best legal structure for your skills and preferences.

If you checked statements 4, 5, and 6, **a partnership** may be the best legal structure for your business.

If you checked statements 2, 4, and 6, you may find that a **corporation** is the best legal structure for your business.

Organizational Considerations

To determine the best structure for your business, you should consider the following organizational questions:

1. How can liability be limited?
2. Should the business be a separate legal entity?
3. How formal should the management and conduct of the business be?
4. How should the organization be structured so that it continues to exist?
5. Is it important for the business interests to be transferred or sold?
6. How expensive will it be to organize the business?
7. What are the guidelines for determining possible sources of operating capital?
8. How will the business taxes be filed?

Each of these questions, and how they impact on the legal status of an organization will be discussed in the following section.

Limited Liability

Persons who start a business are often interested in how they can insulate their personal assets from the operation of the business. Insulating personal assets is most easily accomplished through a limited partnership or a corporation. Regardless of which structure is selected, however, business owners should have insurance that protects personal assets.

Corporation

One of the nontax advantages of the corporation is that it limits liability. Corporate shareholders are usually not liable for the corporation's debts or liabilities. If you start a corporation, however, you should be aware that an investor or financial institution may ask for your personal signature to guarantee payment because of the corporation's limited assets. Although a corporation can protect personal assets, investors might still request that you guarantee the loan personally. If you are unwilling to sign personally for your business, others may question your belief in the success of the business.

Limited Partnership

Partners in a limited partnership are insulated from liability when the partnership's debts are more than the limited partner's capital contribution to the partnership. Thus, a limited partner has less liability than a general partner as long as the limited partner does not participate in the control of the partnership. General partners, who are involved in the management of the business, have the same liability as individuals in a partnership.

Partnership

A partner or a general partner in a limited partnership has unlimited liability. The partnership's assets are first applied to pay the partnership's creditors. In a partnership, however, if the partnership's liabilities exceed assets, the personal assets of each partner can be accessed. Therefore, personal assets such as a home, automobile, savings, and investments all become vulnerable. Furthermore, when a partnership is dissolved, each partner remains liable for the firm's existing obligations. Still another risk in a partnership is that any partner may financially obligate the other partner without the consent of that partner. You become liable for all obligations entered into by any other partner in the business.

Sole Proprietorship

In a sole proprietorship, the individual has unlimited personal liability. Both personal and business assets are subject to claims by creditors. Existing liabilities of a sole proprietor are not dissolved when the business is dissolved or sold.

Separate Legal Entity

A second important consideration is whether the organization will be a separate legal entity and therefore have the right to sue or be sued, to enter into contracts, and to dispose of the firm's assets.

Corporation

A corporation is a separate legal entity and may sue or be sued, hold and receive property, and enter into contracts in its own name. A corporation continues to exist regardless of the status of any shareholder in the corporation. Thus, if a shareholder leaves the corporation or dies, the corporation continues to exist. A corporation is an entity that can be sold because it exists in and of its own right.

Limited Partnership/Partnership

Although common law does not treat a partnership as a separate legal entity, state laws might view a partnership differently. Statutes in many states provide that if a judgment is against one partner, the assets of the sued partner can be tapped, whereas the assets of partners who have not been sued cannot be accessed. This provision varies from state to state, so it is important to know the laws of your state. A partnership ceases to exist whenever one partner leaves the business or dies. The remaining partner or partners must form a new legal structure for the business.

Sole Proprietorship

A sole proprietorship is not a separate legal entity. In some jurisdictions, if the proprietor is married, the spouse's assets can be at risk. Because of this, a spouse should be included in the decision regarding a sole proprietorship. A sole proprietorship ceases to exist at the death of the proprietor.

Formality of Business Conduct

A third consideration is how everyday business will be conducted. That is, you need to determine how formal you want the operation to be.

Corporation

A corporation, including an S Corporation, has central management through a board of directors. The directors are elected by the corporation shareholders, and authority is given to the board to control the corporate policies. The board may consist of a majority of shareholders so that the corporation is actually controlled and managed by the shareholders. In a publicly held corporation, however, the management of the corporation is separate from the corporate ownership.

Managing a corporation requires formalities, many of which are unnecessary in other business forms. The corporation must follow articles of incorporation and bylaws, hold regular meetings of its shareholders and directors, and keep accurate records and minutes of all proceedings. The corporation must also submit additional tax forms and be registered in states where business is conducted. In some instances, an officer must have authorization by the board of directors before taking action.

Limited Partnership

A limited partnership has a centralized form of management like that of a corporation. Management and control of the limited partnership are placed in the hands of the general partners. In many ways, the limited partners are like corporate shareholders because they invest funds and have limited liability. Limited partners also may have a more advantageous tax position because of the way a limited partnership is taxed. A limited partnership is frequently used as a tax shelter in which the limited partners provide capital and the general partners manage the business. A limited partner, however, may lose limited liability if he or she participates in the control of the business.

Partnership

A partnership is like a sole proprietorship to the extent that there are few formal restrictions on how the business is managed. The partners, however, must comply with a partnership agreement. They usually govern the partnership's business affairs by majority vote. The provision of a majority vote ensures that each partner has an equal say in how the partnership is managed. As in a sole proprietorship, there are fewer governmental restrictions and regulations with which the partnership must comply. Although financial statements are not required by the partnership, it must file an information return with the IRS.

Sole Proprietorship

A sole proprietorship does not have to follow formalized procedures in its operation. The proprietor is free to make his or her own decisions and choose the businesses and locations in which he or she wants to operate. The proprietor, therefore, has considerable flexibility in the operation and management of the business.

Continuity of Existence

A fourth consideration is how the business will continue if one of the principals of the business leaves the organization or dies.

Corporation

A corporation is a separate entity. Therefore, it continues to exist regardless of the resignation or death of a principal. A corporation also is not interrupted by the withdrawal or death of a shareholder. Persons forming a corporation, however, need to consider what impact an owner's withdrawal or death may have on the business. Stipulations for leaving the corporation should be stated in a buy/sell agreement.

Limited Partnership

A limited partnership appears to have the perpetual existence of a corporation. However, a limited partnership might exist for only a designated period according to the terms of the partnership agreement. A limited partner may be prohibited from withdrawing contributions until an appointed date. Usually, a limited partner can withdraw his or her contributions if notice is given to the other partners. The amount of notice that must be given to withdraw a contribution is often specified in the partnership agreement. Legal requirements may force the limited partnership to dissolve if this type of withdrawal is made by a limited partner.

The withdrawal or death of a general partner or the sole general partner may cause the limited partnership to dissolve. To prevent dissolution from withdrawal, a certificate of limited partnership may allow a limited partner to substitute a new limited partner in his or her place. To prevent dissolution at the death of a limited partner, the estate of the deceased limited partner may itself become a limited partner and continue in the business.

Partnership

A major disadvantage of a partnership is that the withdrawal of a partner results in the dissolution of the partnership. A partner may withdraw from the partnership, even in direct violation of the partnership agreement. If a partner violates the partnership agreement by leaving, the remaining partners may have the right to buy out the interest of the withdrawing partner. Liquidation might still occur, however, if the remaining partners do not have the funds to complete the buy out.

Sole Proprietorship

If a sole proprietor dies, the business is terminated. To protect the value of the business, however, a sole proprietor may assign in his or her will a personal representative for temporarily operating the business pending liquidation of assets.

Transferability of Interests

A fifth consideration is whether business interests can be transferred or sold.

Corporation

The corporation is the most flexible business form for transferring interests. The organizers of the corporation can divide property into any desired number of shares or classes of shares. The ownership of a corporation is divisible in many ways not available to other forms of business organization.

Limited Partnership

Unless there is a different stipulation in an agreement, a general partner in a limited partnership or a partner in a partnership may transfer partnership interests and grant the rights to the transferee with the consent of all other partners. In this way, the members of the partnership are able to avoid having an unwanted individual thrust on the partnership without their consent. In a limited partnership, the new assignee is given rights to the general partner's share in the profits but is not considered a substitute limited partner. Therefore, the partnership's capital is not interrupted, and the management of the partnership is not altered.

Partnership

As in a limited partnership, a partner can grant the rights to a transferee with the consent of all other partners. The transfer of interests is addressed in the partnership agreement. A new partner, then, cannot be thrust on the existing partners without their consent.

Sole Proprietorship

A sole proprietor has complete freedom to sell or transfer any portion of his or her business assets. Legally, however, there is no business to sell because it doesn't exist without the proprietor.

Expense of Organization

A sixth consideration is the amount of time and money you want to invest in forming a new business.

Corporation

Setting up a corporation can become expensive with the various required fees and start-up costs. Filing a certificate of incorporation involves a filing fee (usually based on the corporation's capital structure). Other possible expenses include fees to set up the formal structure, annual franchise taxes, costs to do business in other states, fees for preparing an annual tax return, and costs for reports required by the state. To keep expenses down, you should incorporate in only those states in which you intend to do business. Hiring an attorney can be an additional expense, but such legal help is advisable. You may find an experienced attorney who can handle the incorporation at a reasonable cost.

Limited Partnership

A limited partnership must follow statutory formalities, and compliance will incur certain expenses. A certificate of limited partnership must be filed, and a written limited partnership agreement must be completed. Costs for fulfilling these requirements will include filing fees and possible legal expenses.

Partnership

A general partnership can usually be organized with little formality or expense. Although not required, a partnership agreement is highly advisable. It protects the interests of all partners and avoids misunderstandings. The development of this agreement may have some costs.

Registration fees are usually required only if the partnership intends to use another name. A general partnership is not required to register in every state in which it intends to do business.

Sole Proprietorship
You can set up a sole proprietorship without any formality or expense unless you intend to do business under an assumed name. There is usually a fee for filing this name.

Sources of Operating Capital

As you think about the right legal structure for your business, a seventh consideration is capital. You need to identify your capital needs, your resources, and other potential sources of capital. If you can provide all of the capital needed to start the business successfully, you can select whatever legal structure meets your other needs and preferences. If, however, your financial resources are limited, you will need to consider your options for getting capital from other sources.

Corporation
The corporation is the most flexible structure for getting operating capital. A corporation can issue common or preferred stock to raise capital. A corporation can also float bonds to acquire capital from the bond purchasers. Later the bonds may be converted into equity. Bonds may have stock warrants or rights attached to them that provide additional incentives to the purchasers. A variety of other types of securities and options may be issued to raise capital for the business.

Limited Partnership
A limited partnership can increase capital resources by using resources from all of the general partners. A major advantage of a limited partnership is that persons can be sought as limited partners who provide capital but do not manage the partnership.

Partnership
A partnership has more options for capitalizing than a sole proprietorship but fewer options than a corporation. Sources of capital include contributions to capital, loans from partners, and loans from outsiders. To increase capital, a partnership can increase its membership. More partners can mean more contributions of capital and more loans to the partnership.

Sole Proprietorship

A sole proprietorship has little flexibility in locating sources for operating capital. Capitalizing is usually limited to individual funds in combination with loans from various sources. Personal assets, however, may be pledged as collateral for loans.

Tax Considerations

Finally, you need to consider taxes before you determine your best form of business organization. One concern is how business taxes will be filed. The ways to report federal income tax vary from one form of organization to the next. This section indicates some tax information you need in order to choose the best legal structure for your business.

Corporation

The income earned by a corporation is taxed at a corporate rate. Once the corporate taxes are paid, each shareholder receives a dividend based on the after-tax earnings of the corporation. The shareholder must then pay individual tax on the dividend. The corporation must pay the employer's share of Social Security tax, and each employee of the corporation matches this share of the tax. Shareholders, however, don't pay self-employment tax on dividends. Therefore, shareholders who work for the corporation may prefer to accept a smaller salary and receive larger dividends.

Subchapter S Corporation

The corporation's payment of corporate taxes and the shareholders' payment of individual taxes on dividends amount to *double taxation*. You can avoid double taxation by filing for Subchapter S status with the IRS. This status allows all income from the corporation to be distributed proportionately among shareholders, and the shareholders then pay personal income tax on their share of income. This arrangement can result in a substantial tax savings. Only those corporations with 35 or fewer shareholders are eligible to receive approval for Subchapter S status.

Limited Partnership and Partnership

The business calculates its income and expenses and then proportions the resulting income or loss among the partners. Federal income tax is paid by the partners at individual tax rates. For Social Security, each general partner pays self-employment tax, which is slightly lower than the amount paid by the corporation and individual combined.

Sole Proprietorship

For tax purposes, the income a sole proprietorship earns is added to any other taxable income of the individual. The IRS has a form for itemizing all business-related expenses. These are deducted from the individual's income. Income taxes are paid by the sole proprietor at the individual rates established by the IRS. No tax is levied against the business itself.

Evaluation of Legal Structure

The following exercise is designed to help you decide which legal structure is best for your new business. Write **I** before each statement that you feel is ***important*** to you. Write **NI** before each statement that you feel is ***not important*** to you.

At the end of each section, you will find a space to place a total. This is calculated by counting the total number of I's (important items) for both the positives and negatives. Deduct the number of I's for the negatives from the number of I's for the positives. Write the result in the space. Compare the total numbers for the proprietorship, partnership, and corporate sections, respectively. The section with the highest total indicates the legal form of business that would be most appropriate for you.

Sole Proprietorship

Positives

_____ Starting a sole proprietorship is easy and quick.

_____ It has few legal requirements or protections.

_____ The owner has complete control over all business decisions.

_____ The owner retains all profits and does not have to share them.

_____ The owner has the satisfaction of running the business alone.

Negatives

_____ You must finance the entire sole proprietorship on your own.

_____ It requires a wide range of management and operational skills.

_____ You are personally liable for all financial obligations of the business.

_____ Tax is not deducted from your salary, and you have no fringe benefits.

_____ The business ceases at your death.

_____ **TOTAL**

Partnership

Positives

_____ A partnership is comparatively easy to establish.

_____ The other partners increase the amount of business and operational expertise.

_____ The other partners provide increased resources for financing the business.

_____ The partners can share responsibility for the business.

_____ The partners can motivate employees by offering them opportunities to become partners in the business.

Negatives

_____ All partners are liable for the business actions of another partner.

_____ Personal assets can be attached to fulfill financial obligations of the business.

_____ Potential disagreements can occur among the partners.

_____ The business has no legal status at the death of a general partner.

_____ It is often difficult for a partner to withdraw and receive any financial remuneration unless the partners buy out the partner.

_____ **TOTAL**

Corporation

Positives

_____ Personal liability for the financial obligations of a corporation is limited.

_____ A multitude of opportunities exist for raising capital for the business.

_____ The business will continue regardless of the withdrawal or death of a major party in the business.

_____ A corporation may have some tax advantages.

_____ It provides for management and operational expertise from active shareholders and the board of directors.

Negatives

_____ A corporation can be costly and difficult to set up.

_____ A corporation must comply with several legal requirements.

_____ What a corporation can do is limited by its charter.

_____ A corporation is restricted in its expansion to other states.

_____ Required public disclosure of financial records restricts secrecy.

_____ **TOTAL**

Summary

Over 70% of all businesses in the United States are sole proprietorships. This makes the sole proprietorship the most popular legal structure.[1] Partnerships account for 10%, and corporations for a little over 19% of all businesses. Corporations, however, generate 90% of all American business revenues. This suggests that a corporation is the most successful form of legal structure because it provides the greatest opportunity for growth.

Endnote

1. U.S. Department of Commerce, *Statistical Abstract of the United States* (Washington, D.C.: U.S. Government Printing Office, 1987), p. 495.

Chapter 5
Writing a Business Plan

Business experts agree that a business plan is an important ingredient to success in any enterprise. A business plan is a document that contains planning information about all aspects of a new enterprise. This chapter tells you why and how to develop a business plan. You learn the basics of a business plan and its main parts. An exercise at the end of the chapter helps you to begin outlining the type of business you might want to start.

Basics of a Business Plan

To develop a business plan for your new venture, you should have some basic perspectives about a business plan. An important preliminary step to creating a business plan is to conduct a feasibility study. This helps you determine at the outset whether the new business you have in mind is workable. It is helpful, too, to know the basic goals of a business plan. To avoid the results of poor planning, you should know also why some entrepreneurs don't plan well when they start a business.

The Feasibility Study

Before you develop a business plan, you need to research your business proposition by completing a feasibility study. This study enables you to make a more informed decision about whether to proceed with the business plan. The study helps you define your objectives so that you can determine the following:

1. Whether your idea for a business is workable.

2. Whether your idea fulfills your objectives in starting a business.

3. Whether your business is likely to succeed in the competitive marketplace.

In developing a feasibility study, you can use the following outline:

I. BUSINESS IDEA REFINEMENT

A. Description of the Business
1. Indicate the competitive edges your business offers.

2. Describe the products or services that will be offered.

3. Describe the customers you plan to target.

4. Briefly describe your operations and distribution of the products.

5. Describe the image you want your business to have and how you plan to achieve this.

B. Specification of Objectives
1. Financial objectives

   a) What are the equity and assets that will help you get your business started?

   b) What collateral can you use?

   c) What is the return on investment that you expect?

   d) What salary do you anticipate drawing for yourself?

2. Satisfaction of personal needs

   a) How will your financial objectives meet your personal needs?

   b) How satisfied are you likely to be in this business venture?

II. ESSENTIAL REQUIREMENTS FOR VENTURE

A. Sufficient Equity/Collateral

B. Ability to Risk Resources

C. Absence of Legal Blockades

1. What licenses, registrations, certificates would block you?

2. What local ordinances and zoning do you need to consider?

3. What might your customer/employee liability be?

D. Suitable Locations

1. What location will provide accessibility and parking?

2. What environmental compliance do you need to remember?

III. VITAL CONSTRAINTS

A. Management Capabilities

1. What technical skills will you need?

2. How does your marketing competence fit what will be required?

3. How sound is your financial understanding of business needs?

4. How competent are you in personnel matters?

5. How well does your management ability fit the plan you would like to develop?

B. Market Determination

1. What are the industry trends?

2. What is your potential target market?

3. What are the customer demographics?

4. What are your sales projections?

5. What kind of competition do you anticipate?

6. What do you expect your market share to be?

7. How will you survey potential consumers to determine the reliability of your business venture?

8. What are your promotional plans?

9. How will you distribute your products or services?

10. Who could your suppliers be?

C. Legal Constraints

1. What are the laws and regulations you need to consider?

2. What legal form of organization would fit your needs?

3. What are the tax implications and possible legal constraints?

4. What constraints might you find regarding trademarks, patents, and copyrights?

5. How might OSHA and labor laws constrain you?

D. Aesthetic and Ethical Considerations

1. What aesthetics are important to you?

2. Do you anticipate any ethical constraints or problems?

E. Physical Development/Capital Budget

1. What land could you use?

2. What building might suit your needs?

3. What furniture and fixtures will you need?

4. What machinery and equipment will be necessary?

5. What kind of inventory will you need?

F. Financial/Operating Budget

1. What kind of financing plan will you need?

2. What equity do you have that will help you with your business venture?

3. What kind of debt must you incur?

4. What would your fixed expenses be?

5. What are the variable/operating expenses you need to consider?

6. What will it take to break even?

7. What will your cash flow needs be?

8. What net and growth net income do you need/desire?

IV. INFORMATION ANALYSIS

A. Objectives

1. Given the information you have uncovered, could you satisfy your personal objectives through this business venture?

2. Given the information you have uncovered, could you meet your financial objectives?

B. Decide Whether to Proceed

Goals of a Business Plan

New business owners tend to act with little thought about the need for planning. A reason is that planning can be hard and tedious work. So that you will be motivated to complete a plan, it is important to understand why planning is necessary. A new venture needs a business plan for three basic reasons.

1. Evaluate success

Developing an entrepreneurial idea can generate much excitement and enthusiasm. With these emotions, you can overlook potential difficulties in starting a business. Such poor planning for growth can become a major roadblock to success.[1] Creating a business plan forces you to examine carefully the business venture you are considering.

2. Provide direction

A business plan provides a blueprint for managing your new business. You can refer to the plan when you face critical decisions. At various points in the growth of your business, you can also compare your actual performance with the plan. If your performance deviates from the plan, you can consider the reasons for the deviations. This type of thoughtful management will help you be more effective in managing the growth of a new business.

3. Obtain financing

A business plan is an absolute requirement for getting outside financing for your business. A study of new software ventures found that companies which did planning grew larger than those that did no planning.[2] Increased growth resulted in greater access to financial resources. Bankers, investors, government agencies, and venture capitalists will expect to see a business plan before they will consider providing financial resources for your business.

Why Entrepreneurs Don't Plan

Knowing why entrepreneurs don't take time to develop a business plan or keep it updated might help you to avoid falling into a similar pattern.

Lack of time

The hectic pace often found in a new business distracts a person from planning. This is one of the reasons for developing a business plan before you start a business. It is then easier to refer to the plan and revise it as necessary.

Procrastination

Many business owners put off planning. One way to ensure planning takes place is to make it a priority for your management activities. Another way is to set a timetable for periodic reviews of your business plan and then stick to the timetable. Assign someone the responsibility for reminding you about the need to plan.

Lack of expertise

A business plan can be a difficult document to create and may require broad expertise in management. If your expertise is limited, the SBA and Small Business Development Centers can help you develop a business plan. Some consultants and accountants also will provide assistance, but for a fee.

Lack of trust

Many entrepreneurs believe that they have a unique idea that must be kept secret for success. They worry about putting their idea in writing for fear that a potential competitor will steal the idea. If this is one of your fears, you might consider using a nondisclosure agreement. An attorney can help you create this document. Then, if someone wants to examine your business plan, you can ask the person to sign a nondisclosure agreement before you reveal your unique idea. A signed nondisclosure agreement is not an absolute guarantee that a person won't steal your idea or reveal elements of your plan to someone else. A signed agreement, however, provides you with stronger legal recourse if the agreement is broken.

Skepticism about value

Many business owners are skeptical about the value of planning. A plan is a goal and doesn't always reflect what is actually done. A plan for a new business often seems like an exercise in speculation. For these reasons, no planning at all is done.

A survey of small businesses found that 48% of failures are caused by lack of capital and 15% by inadequate planning.[3] A lack of capital itself, however, is often the result of poor planning for financial needs and is not simply a reflection of the unwillingness of some bankers to give loans or of investors to buy stock in a new company. The relationship between planning and success should provide some motivation to write a business plan.

Format for a Business Plan

There is no standard format for a business plan. A number of formats are available. The Small Business Administration has a booklet that shows one suggested format. Most banks will suggest their own format if you seek a bank loan. This section presents a format that has been developed from a variety of sources in entrepreneurial literature.

Here are the major sections you will most often find in a business plan:

1. Executive Summary

2. Mission Statement, Goals, Objectives, and Strategies

3. Marketing Plan

4. Design and Development Plan

5. Operations or Manufacturing Plan

6. Principal Parties

7. Work Plan and Schedule

8. Potential Problems and Risks

9. Benefits to the Community

10. Financial Plan

These parts of a business plan are discussed in the following sections. You can use this information to develop a sound plan for your business venture. Space is provided so that you can jot down responses to questions and statements as you read about these parts of a business plan. If you are not prepared to offer responses at this stage of your investigation, a brief exercise at the end of this chapter will help you start the process of creating a business plan that you can later develop in detail.

Executive Summary

An executive summary provides an overview of a business plan that can be given to potential investors, key people, and financial organizations. The executive summary should be informative and entice the reader to go further into the document. This summary, which should not exceed five pages, should appear at the beginning of the business plan and be a separate document to be read first. The executive summary should be a concise statement of the plan, providing highlights and features. By reading just the executive summary, an individual should be able to preview the business plan quickly and understand its intent. The executive summary should be well written so that it adequately represents the tone and depth of the full document.

The following information can be included in an executive summary. In the space provided, you may make notes regarding the executive summary you would write. Once you have reviewed this chapter and determined that you would like to write a business plan in earnest, you can return to these pages to make notes for the executive summary you could write.

Background

Indicate the date your company was formed and explain why it was formed. Name the principal parties and mention the problems you are trying to solve. Indicate also the audience you plan to serve.

_____

_____

_____

_____

_____

_____

_____

Market research and analysis

Describe the size and growth rate of the market that you believe is ready for your product or service. Give an overview of industry trends and future projections that show the opportunity for your product or service.

_____

_____

_____

_____

_____

_____

_____

Product, service, and technical information

Briefly describe the product or service offered by your business, showing how the product or service is unique. What competitive edge will it have in the marketplace? What technology will be used in production? What technical skills do key individuals have?

_____

_____

_____

_____

_____

_____

Financial projection

Provide an overview of the sales and profit projections for the first one to two years of operation. The reader should have an idea of how profitable the business might be during a two-year period.

_____

_____

_____

_____

_____

_____

Competition

Identify your key competitors, explaining why people now buy from them. Indicate the strengths and weaknesses of your major competitors' products or services. Compare your product or service with those of your competitors, stating your advantages and price differences. Show how your product or service will be perceived by potential customers and why they will prefer your product to those of your competitors.

_____

_____

_____

_____

_____

_____

_____

Estimated market share

Provide a percentage estimate of the market share that you believe your product or service can achieve during short- and long-term periods. Support your projections with facts or other information.

_____

_____

_____

_____

_____

_____

Continual market evaluation

Indicate how you will keep abreast of what happens in the marketplace. Show how you plan to monitor your product or service as well as competitive products or services. Explain how you will stay informed of issues affecting your product or service and its market.

_____

_____

_____

_____

_____

_____

_____

Mission Statement, Goals, Objectives, and Strategies

Strategic planning principles should guide your business plan. It should include statements about four issues commonly associated with strategic planning: mission, goals, objectives, and strategies. These statements should display a sound understanding of your business and the results of its implementation and operation. Other issues that are generally addressed might include trends, environmental scan, and market niche.

Mission statement

Explain in one paragraph the reason or purpose of your business. Indicate the product or service your business will provide. Describe the chief customers of your business.

_____

_____

_____

_____

Goals

A *goal* is a one-sentence statement of what you intend to accomplish with your business within three to five years. Goals guide the progress of your business.

Objectives

An *objective* is a one-sentence statement about a specific benchmark you intend to achieve with your business in the fulfillment of a goal. (A benchmark is a point of reference for measuring progress.) Each goal may have three to five objectives. Usually, objectives are set yearly.

Strategies

A *strategy* is a one-sentence statement that indicates how to achieve an objective. Each objective may have several strategies.

Use the following table to indicate your chief goals, your objectives to achieve these goals, and your strategies to accomplish these objectives.

Goals	Objectives	Strategies
A.	1.	a)
		b)
	2.	a)
		b)
	3.	a)
		b)
B.	1.	a)
		b)
	2.	a)
		b)
	3.	a)
		b)

Marketing Plan

When you develop the marketing section of your business plan, you should consider three issues: the industry, the market, and marketing strategy. Because this book is presented in a workbook format, space is provided for you to indicate answers to questions about these issues. If you decide to become an entrepreneur, you can return to these pages to complete your initial planning in more detail.

Industry analysis

First, you should analyze the industry to find out about its history and any future trends that will affect the business you intend to start. Consider the following questions and use the space to indicate your responses.

1. What position will your product or service have in the industry? That is, what needs will your product or service satisfy?

    _____

    _____

    _____

2. What major developments will affect the industry and customers?

    _____

    _____

    _____

3. What social, political, and economic trends will affect your business?

    _____

    _____

    _____

Market research

Another critical task is the analysis of the market to be served by your business. This market may be local, regional, state, multistate, or national. Researching your competition and understanding how to compete effectively in the market are important. Business schools are often willing to conduct this type of research, using graduate students at a low cost.Address these questions:

1. Who are the potential customers for your product or service?

   _____

   _____

2. Why will they buy your product or service?

   _____

   _____

3. What is the geographic area of your market?

   _____

   _____

4. What is the market's size?

   _____

   _____

5. What are the market trends?

   _____

   _____

6. Who are your competitors?

   _____

   _____

7. What is your potential for growth?

   _____

   _____

Market strategy

Third, you should consider the strategies you will use to market your product or service. What will be the price of your product or service? Who will manage sales and advertising? What will be your policies on service and credit? You should consider all of the following issues as you devise an effective marketing plan.

Pricing strategy. This part of the plan explains how you will price your product or service and whether your price will enable your business to compete effectively. Respond to these questions:

1. How will you price your product or service?

   _____

   _____

2. How will you determine whether your price is competitive?

   _____

   _____

3. How will you continually review your pricing to remain competitive?

   _____

   _____

Sales strategies. Here are the strategies you will use to sell your product or service. Consider the following questions:

1. Who are the key employees in the sales area?

   _____

   _____

2. Where will you target your sales?

   _____

   _____

3. How successful do you expect your strategies to be?

   _____

   _____

Service and warranty policies. An important aspect of marketing is determining the policies about the service you provide, or the warranty and service that cover the product you sell. Be sure to address the following questions:

1. What maintenance guarantee will your customers receive?

   _____

   _____

2. How do you propose to give maximum service and keep costs down?

   _____

   _____

3. What will you do to ensure ongoing maintenance for customers?

   _____

   _____

Advertising/Promotion plan. Explain how you plan to advertise or promote your product or service. Consider these questions:

1. What will be the primary means of advertising?

   _____

   _____

2. Who will be responsible for advertising and promotion?

   _____

   _____

3. What are the key elements of your plan?

   _____

   _____

Credit policies. Describe the policies for extending credit to customers. Consider the following questions:

1. What type of credit will you extend?

_____

_____

2. How will you determine interest rates?

_____

_____

3. What methods will you use to determine credit risk?

_____

_____

Design and Development Plan

If your product or service requires design and development, you should have a plan for these tasks. Investors, in particular, will want to know the nature and extent of design and development, as well as the costs and time frame for completion before the product or service is marketable.

Status

Describe the status of the product or service. Indicate what needs to be done before the product or service is marketable. Address the following questions:

1. How will you make a prototype for the product?

_____

_____

2. How will you test the product to determine whether it is safe and effective?

_____

_____

3. How will you field-test the product before it can be marketed?

_____

_____

4. Who will take responsibility for developing the product or service?

_____

_____

5. How much technical assistance will you need before the product or service is marketable?

_____

_____

Problems and risk

Indicate problems that could occur during the design or development stage. Discuss how these difficulties might impede design or development and increase costs. In other words, show the degree of risk involved with the design or development phase.

_____

_____

_____

_____

_____

_____

_____

_____

_____

_____

_____

Tasks to be completed

State the tasks that need to be completed before the design or development phase is completed. Consider these questions:

1. What additional design or development is needed before the product is complete?

   _____

   _____

2. How much design or development is needed before the product is competitive?

   _____

   _____

3. What additional products or services could be developed?

   _____

   _____

Costs

Use separate sheets to plan in more detail a budget for the design and development phase. Be sure to include costs for labor, materials, consulting fees, and production of a prototype. Be realistic about the costs of this phase. You also should document your cost estimates.

Operations or Manufacturing Plan

This section of the plan shows how your business will be designed and operated.

Manufacturing

If your venture includes the manufacturing of a product, you need to develop a manufacturing plan. This plan should address the following questions:

1. What kind of facility will your business need?

   _____

   _____

2. What is the preferred location for the facility?

_____

_____

3. What are the space requirements within the facility?

_____

_____

4. What manufacturing process will be used?

_____

_____

5. What specific types of equipment will be required?

_____

_____

6. How much equipment will be required?

_____

_____

Service

If your business provides a service, you need to describe the service and show how you will provide it. Your description should address the following questions:

1. What type of facility is needed?

_____

_____

2. What methods will be used to provide the service?

_____

_____

3. What equipment is required to provide the service?

_____

_____

Geographic location

Describe the preferred location for the business, taking into consideration the following questions:

1. What states offer the greatest advantages in state and local tax laws?

   _____

   _____

2. How near will your operation be to the marketplace?

   _____

   _____

3. How accessible are interstates and other highways for transportation of the product?

   _____

   _____

4. What will be the cost of utilities?

   _____

   _____

5. What are the zoning laws?

   _____

   _____

Facilities

Consider whether you can use an existing facility for your business or whether you must construct a new facility. When identifying potential facilities, consider the following requirements:

1. What amount of space is required (for both the plant and office)?

   _____

   _____

2. What amount of land is needed?

_____

_____

3. What amount of storage is needed?

_____

_____

As you consider facilities, be sure to answer the following questions:

1. Will constructing a new facility be more expensive than using an existing facility?

_____

_____

2. Will constructing a new facility take longer than renovating an existing facility?

_____

_____

3. Will building a new facility provide greater tax advantages than renovating an existing facility?

_____

_____

Labor force

In developing an operations plan, consider the labor force you will require to produce your product or service. Address these questions:

1. What skill levels must the workers have to produce your goods or provide your services successfully?

_____

_____

2. What labor force with the desired skill level and wage rates is available in the geographical area?

_____

_____

3. Historically, what has been the relationship between management and labor in this geographical area?

_____

_____

4. What is the work ethic like in the area you are considering? How well do the work habits and attitudes of workers in the geographical area fit your requirements or expectations?

_____

_____

5. What are the competitive wage rates for the local area?

_____

_____

6. What training and educational programs are available in the area to upgrade skills and keep the labor force competitive?

_____

_____

7. How available are consultants or specialists who are necessary for the manufacturing of your product?

_____

_____

Principal Parties

The business plan should describe the principal parties involved in the business venture. Investors will want to know the experience, skills, and technical expertise of the management team.

Description of key individuals

Begin by discussing the human resource needs of your business venture. Indicate what individuals will be required in the following areas (if they are included in the plan):

1. Production of your product

    _____

    _____

2. Marketing of your product or service

    _____

    _____

3. Overall management

    _____

    _____

4. Accounting or financial management

    _____

    _____

5. Management of the labor force

    _____

    _____

6. Members of the board of directors

    _____

    _____

7. Principal partners

    _____

    _____

8. Management personnel

    _____

    _____

If you use your business plan to get financing, you should include in an appendix to your plan a resume for each key person in the organization.

Organizational chart

Describe the organizational structure of your business. Show who the key players will be and what the reporting structure will be like. Your discussion can be general, but it should be clear that you have analyzed the organizational structure of your business.

_____

_____

_____

_____

_____

_____

Compensation plan

Indicate the starting salaries for each of the key parties and compare these salaries with comparable salaries in the marketplace. If individuals will be working for less than the local wage rate, explain why they will be willing to work for less. Specify any fringe benefits you plan to offer.

_____

_____

_____

_____

_____

_____

Board of directors

If your business will have a board of directors, discuss the size and composition of the board and how members will be selected.

_____

_____

_____

_____

_____

_____

Human resource management

Describe the management of human resources, including the recruiting, training, and supervising of staff. If you plan to use special training programs (such as state-sponsored programs), discuss how these programs will be identified and utilized.

_____

_____

_____

_____

_____

_____

Work Plan and Schedule

Provide a general time line for the start-up of your business. For the work plan, specify a time frame for the completion of each task and indicate who will be responsible for completing each task. You should include the following milestones:

Formalizing structure (other than incorporating)

_____

_____

_____

Completion of the design and development of the product or service

_____

_____

_____

Completion of a prototype (if there is one)

_____

_____

_____

Recruitment of key personnel

_____

_____

_____

Development of sales and marketing plan

_____

_____

_____

Acquisition of facility

_____

_____

_____

Ordering of supplies and materials

_____

_____

_____

Start-up of production or operation

_____

_____

_____

Estimate of delivery of product or service

_____

_____

_____

Start date for sales

_____

_____

_____

Potential Problems and Risks

A valuable exercise is to anticipate problems you may have during the start-up of your business. You should identify potential risks as well as possible problem areas. In your discussion, explain how you might resolve these problems or risks. Investors will want to know that you have anticipated such problems and are prepared to deal with them as they occur. You might consider the following potential problems:

Price differential between your product or service and those of your competitors

_____

_____

_____

Unfavorable industry-wide trends and their effect on your business plan

_____

_____

_____

Unforeseen competition

_____

_____

_____

Problems in the design and development stage

_____

_____

_____

Difficulties during initial production phase

_____

_____

_____

Higher development costs than were expected

_____

_____

_____

Difficulty in finding trained workers or key individuals

_____

_____

_____

Benefits to the Community

Discuss how your business will benefit the community in which you are living or working. Investors will want to see how your business will especially benefit them or their community. This will be an important issue if you seek government loans, grants, or tax deferments. Describe the potential economic or quality-of-life benefits you foresee. These might include the following:

Increased number of jobs in the community

_____

_____

_____

Increased number of skilled or higher-paying jobs

_____

_____

_____

New technical skills developed within the work force

_____

_____

_____

Increased number of residents in the community who will benefit from the new jobs

_____

_____

_____

More people drawn to the community because of the product or service

_____

_____

_____

New taxes generated in the community

_____

_____

_____

Additional community support from employees of the new business

_____

_____

_____

Financial Plan

The financial section is one of the most important parts of a business plan. The reason many businesses fail is due to unrealistic financial projections. Make certain that the data you gather for this section of your business plan is both accurate and realistic. Investors will especially want to know how you plan to finance your new business and how realistic your projections are. The financial plan should include in detail the following sections:

1. Operating Budget

2. Profit and Loss Forecast for a Three-Year Period

3. Cash Flow Projections for Three Years

4. Balance Sheets for Start-up, First Year, and the End of the First Three Years of Operation

Many banks will suggest specific formats for a financial plan. If you have access to a personal computer with a spreadsheet program, you can find ready-made templates or worksheets for these financial reports. If you are not an expert at finances and accounting, you might want to hire a certified public accountant (CPA) to help you develop this part of your business plan.

Start-up and operating costs

Some start-up and operating costs are standard from one business to another. The following list may help you anticipate these costs. Write your projected amounts in the space provided.

1. Professional fees _____

2. Organizational fees _____

3. Furniture and fixtures _____

4. Equipment and machinery _____

5. Deposits _____

6. Supplies _____

7. Insurance _____

8. Advertising _____

9. Working capital _____

10. Employee recruitment and training _____

11. Inventory _____

12. Building renovations _____

Many experts suggest that a new business venture should have a minimum of six months cash on hand. An entrepreneur needs enough money to get started and to cover anticipated costs. An entrepreneur needs also to know where to find six months of income should it not be produced by the new business venture.

Getting Started on a Business Plan

If you were not ready to provide information in most of the blank spaces throughout this chapter, this brief exercise will help you get started on a business plan for your new venture. You can use this information later as a springboard to develop a sound and thorough document.

1. Summarize briefly the type of business you would like to start.

   _____

   _____

   _____

2. Indicate the purpose of the business and the product or service to be provided.

   _____

   _____

   _____

3. What do you know about the market for your product or service? What else will you need to know? Why do you think you could sell your product or service?

   _____

   _____

   _____

4. What kind of design and development will be needed for your product or service before you can market it?

   _____

   _____

   _____

5. What will be your need for manufacturing facilities and employees? Where would you locate your business and why?

_____

_____

_____

6. Who would you want or need to have as partners, investors, or key persons?

_____

_____

_____

7. How will you develop a work plan that covers the time from start-up to the start date for sales?

_____

_____

_____

8. What problems and risks can you expect in starting the business?

_____

_____

_____

9. How will your new business benefit the community?

_____

_____

_____

10. What amount of financing do you think would be needed for the business? Where might you get the necessary financing?

_____

_____

_____

Later, when you are ready to develop a thorough business plan, you can return to the main sections of this chapter and provide detailed responses to specific questions that are relevant to your particular new venture.

Summary

A business plan is a key planning and financing instrument for a new business venture. The purpose of the plan is to generate information for the sake of developing the plan. The Small Business Administration has some excellent materials on how to develop a business plan. In your early research, find examples of business plans.

Endnotes

1. Leon C. Megginson, Charles R. Scott, and William L. Megginson, *Successful Small Business Management* (Homewood, IL: Irwin, 1991), p. 72.

2. Richard D. Teach, Fred A. Tarpley, Jr., Robert G. Schwartz, and Dorothy E. Brawley, "Maturation in the Microcomputer Software Industry: Venture Teams and Their Firms," in Churchill and others, *Frontiers of Entrepreneurship* (Wellesley, MA: Babson Center for Entrepreneurial Studies, 1987), p. 464.

3. *USA Today,* March 13, 1987, p. 13, as derived from Minolta Corporation's January 1987, survey of 703 businesses with fewer than 500 employees.

Chapter 6
Financing Your Business

When you start a business, the most critical factor is the initial capitalization. You learned in the preceding chapter that completing a business plan is important for financing your new business successfully. A business plan helps you determine the amount of money your business will need during its first few years of operation. You can thus avoid failure due to insufficient finances. Furthermore, the sources you approach for funds for your business usually require that you have a business plan. In this chapter, you learn what sources of funds are available to begin a business.

A survey found that when businesses are started, the top three preferred sources of financing are venture capital (28%), no outside financing (20%), and banks (18.7%). After businesses have been in operation for five years, the top three preferences are public offerings (43.1%), banks (19%), and no outside financing (12.1%).[1] This information may be useful to you as you examine the following sources of financing for your business.

Personal Resources

Many personal resources are usually available to start a business. Relying on such resources is sometimes called *bootstrap financing*. You need to be prepared to risk your own money, assets, and time to start the business. Few, if any, investors will want to invest in a business in which the owner has not invested personal money. The following items provide you with some ideas for bootstrap financing.

Savings
Personal savings are the easiest funds to obtain for a new business. Usually, you can withdraw them immediately.

Life insurance cash values
If your life insurance has cash surrender values, you can cash in policies for the cash values, or you can borrow them to raise cash for your new business. You should realize, however, that you reduce your protection by the amount of the loan, and you will pay interest on the amount you borrow. Usually, there is a waiting period before you can get cash this way.

Withdrawals from investments or retirement funds
Investments in stocks, mutual funds, or real estate may be available to you, but these resources are more difficult to get quickly. Some retirement plans allow a person to have a cash settlement. An Individual Retirement Account (IRA) also can be cashed. Keep in mind, however, that IRAs and other kinds of tax-deferred investments and retirement plans may have penalties for early withdrawal. Furthermore, the government will assess income tax on money withdrawn from retirement funds.

Home mortgages
You may be able to mortgage your home or take a second mortgage. Funds from this resource can be obtained more readily than some investments if your bank is cooperative. Be aware, though, that a second mortgage may put your house at risk if your new venture proves unsuccessful.

Relatives and friends
Some people borrow money from relatives and friends to start a business. If you value the relationship you have with these people, you should never borrow money without signing a legal note. Be prepared to repay this loan regardless of the success of your business. You also might feel obligated to guarantee a portion of the profits from the business to the person giving you the loan.

Contract from former employer

A potential source for financing might be your former employer. This would probably not be actual money but a contract for your product or service. A banker will normally be willing to provide a loan for operating capital based on such a contract.

Initial contracts with new customers

You might be able to provide a product or service that another business needs. In such a case, the business should be willing to give you a contract that you can use to raise operating capital through a bank loan.

Vendors

You might find suppliers who will advance you credit. This provides you with a short-term loan. The suppliers' products are at your disposal to generate sales before you have to pay for the products. Not all vendors will advance credit to a new business, so you may want to select only those suppliers who will do so.

Personal Resources Checklist

As you consider financing from personal resources, use the following checklist to help you decide how you might finance your business. Check only those resources that you have and are willing to use to invest in your business.

_____ I have savings in a savings account that I could use to start the business.

_____ I have stocks and mutual funds that I could sell to start the business.

_____ I have property or real estate that I could sell to get financing.

_____ I could get cash from a retirement fund.

_____ I could borrow money against a retirement fund or life insurance policy.

_____ I could get a mortgage or home loan.

_____ I have relatives and friends who would invest in the business or lend me the money.

_____ I know a former employer who would sign a contract with my new business.

_____ I know business acquaintances who would sign a contract with my new business.

A question that you must ask yourself is how much you are willing to risk in personal assets to go into business. List the resources you would invest.

_____   _____

_____   _____

_____   _____

_____   _____

What percent of your total assets would you be willing to invest in your business?

_____ %

Equity

Another method for raising the necessary finances for your business is to give investors equity in the business in return for their cash investment. This approach has both advantages and disadvantages, some of which are listed here.

Increased financial capacity
It is possible to raise much more money through investors than can be raised individually or through a small group of partners.

Greater credit
A lending institution is more likely to provide loans to a business that is backed by a group of strong investors.

Less control
You obviously lose some control over the business after you acquire investors. They will typically want voting stock, and this will allow them to elect members of the board of directors. You can sell less than 50%

of the stock and retain a majority share in the business, but you will no longer have the full control of total ownership.

Less profit
Investors will share in all profits from the business. In the first few years of operation, sharing profits is seldom much of an issue. As the business prospers, however, you might come to regret having sold shares in your company.

Additional legal requirements
State and federal laws govern the sale of stock in a company. You will need to research the laws in your state. Before you seek investors, it is advisable to hire an attorney to ensure that you meet all state and federal laws and regulations.

Pressure from shareholders
Investors will expect to receive dividends from their investment. This expectation will put pressure on you to produce a profit as quickly as possible. A new business, however, needs to reinvest in itself. Some investors might not understand this need and will grow unhappy about not receiving a return on their investment.

Raising Equity Capital

There are many ways to raise capital through investors. It is not advisable, though, to use any of the following methods without the counsel of an attorney. As you evaluate these methods, you should recognize several factors:

1. The amount of money that you can raise is directly related to the number of available investors. However, when you make shares available to a large number of people, the legal requirements and accompanying expense increase.

2. The amount of equity that you make available is critical. The more equity the shareholders purchase, the less profit and control you keep as the owner. But if you retain too much control or too high a percentage of equity, many investors will be reluctant to invest.

3. The geographic area to which you direct your search for investors is significant. When you cross state boundaries, meeting state and federal laws and regulations becomes more complicated.

Corporations might raise funds through the sale of stock. The methods for raising equity through stock sales are explained in the following paragraphs. Keep the preceding factors in mind when you read these explanations.

Intrastate stock sale

It is possible to sell stocks in just one state. When this is done, the corporation must comply with the regulations of that state. To sell stock, the management must disclose sufficient information to the investors to allow them to make informed decisions. Both private placement of stock and public offerings may take place in intrastate transactions.

Private placement

A private placement is regulated by state and federal laws. Some general guidelines apply to this type of offering. The number of shareholders is usually limited to no more than 35 nonaccredited purchasers. (There is a lengthy legal definition of accredited purchasers.) Furthermore, the amount of money that can be raised is limited. If investors are solicited from more than one state, interstate regulations apply. Nevertheless, a private placement has certain advantages. It is less cumbersome than a public offering. With a private placement of stock, there is no immediate need for payback. The capital can therefore be used to develop the new business.

Public offering

Raising funds by offering stock to the public is not as desirable for a start-up business. For a public offering, a company must demonstrate that it can provide investors with a good return on their investment. The business must not only show financial strength but also find an underwriter that will help in selling the stock. When the stock is sold to the public, the business has no control over who invests in the business. For even a strong start-up business with friendly investors, the amount of capital that is raised from a public offering depends on the health of the stock market at the time of the offering.

Venture capital

A venture capital firm consists of individuals who invest funds in new or rapidly growing businesses. Because new ventures contain a high degree of risk, a venture capital firm expects a high rate of return for its investment. Such firms expect a large percentage (perhaps as high as 50%) of the business in return for the funds they invest. You can identify venture capital firms through bankers, attorneys, and state agencies. Getting venture capital for new firms, however, is becoming increasingly difficult.

Small Business Investment Corporations (SBICs)

An SBIC is a venture capital firm that is licensed by the Small Business Administration. The SBIC must raise private money and can then use it to borrow additional funds from the SBA. SBICs operate much like regular venture capital firms and will expect a high rate of return for their investment.

State and local governments

Some states, counties, and cities have established funds for investing in new businesses. Usually, these programs are created with the idea of promoting a specific type of business—for example, high-tech businesses, labor-intensive businesses, or businesses that will locate in economically depressed areas. You need to contact your local Small Business Development Center for help in identifying such programs in your area.

Loans

The owner of a new business may be able to get a loan for the business. Most lending institutions grant loans for specific purposes. For that reason, you may have difficulty in getting a loan for *working capital*. This refers to the funds that a business needs for paying its daily bills and meeting payroll. Lending institutions are likely to give a loan for the four purposes described here.

Equipment purchase loan

Obtaining equipment for an office, a store, or a manufacturing operation is often possible because the lending institution can place a lien against the equipment. A lien is a legal hold on property which can result in the sale of such property for payment to satisfy a debt. The judgment about whether to make a loan is usually based on the potential for the lending institution to resell the equipment. Ordinarily, a loan is for the expected life of the equipment, as determined by a depreciation schedule.

Inventory loan
A lending institution might be willing to give the credit necessary to purchase inventory. When used by retailers, this credit is called floor planning. In essence, the lending institution owns the inventory. As items are sold, the loan is repaid. This type of loan is usually a short-term loan.

Buildings loan
A bank might be willing to provide a loan for a building that it would secure with a mortgage. This type of loan would probably be for a long term (20+ years).

Accounts receivable loan
The accounts receivable of a business can often be used to get a loan. The lending institution speculates that most accounts will be paid and the business will be able to repay the loan. This is the same rationale used for lending when a business has a contract for services or products. The contract provides a high degree of probability that a business will earn the money necessary to repay the loan.

Loans for Working Capital

Although loans given for specific purposes are usually quite helpful to a new business, most businesses need capital to provide for their working needs. The following sources are among those that offer loans for capital.

Lending institution line of credit
It is possible to get a loan from a bank or commercial finance company. However, both the lender and the borrower will benefit from using a method known as a *line of credit*. This is the maximum amount of money that the borrower may borrow from the lending institution. The borrower draws on the line of credit only as the money is needed. Suppose, for example, that a bank approves a line of credit for $100,000. The business might need only $20,000 in October, so $20,000 is the

amount actually obtained from the bank. This limits the company's liability as well as reduces the amount of interest that must be paid.

Small Business Administration guaranteed loan programs

These programs provide guarantees to banks that lend to approved small businesses. The SBA guarantees coverage of from 70% to 90% of a loan, depending on the amount. The programs are intended to provide banks with incentives to make loans to small businesses. You can find out about these programs by contacting a local banker who works with or through the SBA.

Certified Development Company (CDC) loan program

The purpose of the Certified Development Company loan program (503 Loan Program) is to help small businesses by providing long-term fixed asset financing. Loan proceeds might be used for the purchase of land, buildings, new construction, expansion, or machinery and equipment.

The financing package for a CDC loan is structured as follows. Fifty percent is from the participating bank (of the applicant's choice) at the bank's interest rate and terms. The bank takes a first mortgage. Forty percent is from a CDC debenture, guaranteed 100% by the Small Business Administration. The remaining 10% is through equity or business investment by the owner(s).

Federal Farmers Home Administration

To promote economic development of small businesses in rural areas, the FHA provides loan guarantees of up to 90% of the value of a loan.

State and local government programs

Many state and local governments have loan programs. These often are designed to promote specific government goals and policies.

Lenders' Criteria
for Business Loans

Lending institutions are usually conservative in their decisions. They expect a business to demonstrate a high probability that it will repay a loan. The following points are normally considered by lending institutions.

Business concept (business plan)

Your business plan is important to a lender. It displays a well-planned approach to business. Furthermore, it provides a tangible basis for deciding whether a loan is likely to be repaid.

Collateral

The lender might require collateral to secure the loan. The lender does this by holding a lien against buildings, equipment, inventory, or other assets.

Down payment

The lender might require a down payment on the loan. Normally, this money must come from the principal(s) in the business. The percentage of down payment varies from one lender to another.

Credit record

A new business does not have a credit record. Therefore, a lender will examine the credit history of the principals in the company. You may need to secure a loan by pledging your personal assets. To make a decision, a lender may require a statement of your personal financial net worth.

Management ability

In deciding whether to grant you a loan, a lender will examine your management ability. This is evident in your work experience and business plan.

Considerations for a Financing Option

A decision about which financing option you will use must be based on the following considerations:

Availability

You might have a limited choice in financing options. The availability of capital from outside resources will vary with the general health of the economy, as well as that of your local area. Investors will be more likely to purchase stock when the economy is good. Government funds are usually more plentiful at the beginning and end of a fiscal year.

Repayment

A loan must be repaid with interest. You might be required to secure a loan with your personal assets, possibly taking on considerable financial risk. Shareholders do not have to be repaid.

Control

A lender will expect you to follow prudent management principles. Investors, however, will become more involved in decisions for the business. They will elect members to the board of directors and will serve as directors. An owner thus loses some control over the business when selling shares in it.

Government Grants

Chapter 1 discussed several programs that are available from the state and federal governments to assist small business start-ups. You may want to review these programs as possible sources for financial assistance.

Financial Assessment Exercise

Answer the following questions by filling in the blanks or checking the appropriate answers.

1. Approximately how much money will you need to start your business?

   $_____

2. How would you prefer to obtain financing for your business?

   _____ Bootstrap financing   _____ Investors

   _____ Venture capital   _____ Government grants

   _____ Government loans   _____ Commercial loans

3. What were your reasons for selecting the preceding sources for financial capital?

   _____

   _____

   _____

4. Which sources are most likely to provide you the money?

_____ Bootstrap financing   _____ Investors

_____ Venture capital   _____ Government grants

_____ Government loans   _____ Commercial loans

5. What are your reasons for your answers to the preceding question?

_____

_____

_____

Summary

Financing a business is extremely critical. Your success depends on the availability of sufficient capital for you to carry out the business plan. Not having the money necessary to conduct business operations correctly can be an extremely frustrating experience. Moreover, this type of problem frequently leads to failure. Before going into business, you should identify sufficient capital to ensure your success.

Endnote

1. Albert V. Bruno and Tyzoon T. Tyebjee, "The Entrepreneur's Search for Capital," *Journal of Business Venturing* (Winter 1985), p. 71.

Chapter 7
The Business Team

An entrepreneur should identify and build a team of key professionals who can help establish the business structure and operation. Every entrepreneur should seriously consider engaging an attorney, a certified public accountant, a banker, an insurance agent, and consultants as needed. These professionals can provide expertise and advice for the new business.

Many entrepreneurs are tempted to avoid the expenses of the services of these professionals, but this investment is necessary in starting a business. If you don't get the help of these professionals when you start your business, you might pay far more monetarily and emotionally as your business grows. Interview at least three candidates before selecting the members of your team. Most professionals will give you an hour of free time for this purpose. Discuss the nature of your visit and clarify charges before setting the appointment.

Members of the Business Team

As an entrepreneur, you face two major issues when starting a business. First, many federal, state, and local laws and regulations directly affect the operation of a business and must be observed. Second, Americans like to sue. If you want your business to be successful, you must protect it against potential lawsuits. An attorney will help you manage your business lawfully and therefore reduce the chance of a lawsuit. In an

INC. magazine survey of about 5,000 readers, 94% reported that they customarily seek the help of an attorney.[1]

Attorney

Initially, the attorney performs a critical function for your business. An attorney helps you structure the business appropriately, files all the necessary legal documents, and advises you on licenses you must get and zoning ordinances you must follow. The attorney thus helps you set up the legal foundation of your business. Retaining the services of an attorney before you start your business can help you avoid many problems over the years. This can save you time, money, and effort to correct legal problems you may create by starting the business without legal assistance.

It is possible to find attorneys who will help you establish your business for a reasonable fee. You should expect legal assistance with the following matters.

Legal structure

An attorney will advise you on the best legal structure for your business. A partnership or limited partnership should have a formal agreement about the operation of the business. The attorney should prepare such an agreement. If your business is to be a corporation, formal papers must be submitted to the state for incorporation, and corporate bylaws must be written. The attorney can complete these tasks and get stock certificates, a corporate seal, and a corporate record book, which are usually required by state law for a corporation.

Franchising and licensing

An attorney should review any type of licensing or franchise agreement that you sign. This should protect you from problems you cannot foresee. In addition, the attorney can explain the aspects of a franchise that are to your benefit, as well as those that benefit the franchisor.

Patents, trademarks, and copyrights

The protection of intellectual property is a vital part of business law in a competitive society. An invention is protected by a patent. A trademark is a word, name, symbol, or device used by a business to differentiate itself or a product from the rest of the market. A copyright protects written property and computer software. The practice of patent, trademark, and copyright law is highly technical. Your local attorney can identify reliable attorneys who specialize in this field of law. If you want to get a patent, you should seek the help of a patent attorney because of the technicalities connected with this process.

Contracts and agreements

Frequently, you will be involved in making business arrangements with other organizations. Such arrangements need to be formalized with a contract or agreement. You should ask an attorney to prepare the contract or review a contract presented by another business. You should never sign a contract without the review of an attorney.

Federal and state reports

It is advisable to have your attorney prepare or review reports that you must make to federal and state governments that affect the legal status of your business.

General legal matters

During the operation of a business, many issues arise that have legal implications. For example, terminating an employee, having an employee sign a noncompetition agreement, and complying with city ordinances are matters for which you will need legal advice.

Establishing a professional relationship with an attorney at the start of your business thus ensures that you are in compliance with all laws and regulations. The attorney will become familiar with your business and will be prepared to offer informed advice should a legal issue arise that requires an attorney's assistance.

Certified Public Accountant

A certified public accountant (CPA) can provide important advice in the operation of your business. This member of your business team is particularly important if you need help with accounting or tax preparation. You will find that an accountant is useful for the following reasons.

Legal structure

A CPA can help you choose the type of legal structure that will be most beneficial from a tax perspective.

Government forms and filings

A CPA can help you comply with many government requirements. If you choose to incorporate your business, the CPA can help you file for Subchapter S status. If you hire employees, you must obtain an employer identification number from the IRS. You must also prepare numerous forms for the IRS, state revenue services, and state employment services. The CPA can either prepare the reports or provide guidance as you prepare them. The CPA can also answer questions about these reports if the IRS makes any inquiries.

Accounting procedures

A CPA can help you choose the method of bookkeeping for your business. Many CPAs know of computer software programs that can maintain your financial records. An important aspect of accounting assistance is determining the chart of accounts that will be used in the bookkeeping for your business.

Tax preparation

A CPA can prepare the tax returns for your business. Tax regulations and tax court interpretations result in numerous changes in tax preparation from one year to the next. Unless you keep abreast of these changes, you can make a mistake or overlook a tax advantage for the business.

Audits

A CPA can conduct an annual audit of your business if the volume of business is large in dollars. Publicly held corporations must obtain audits to disclose financial information to the shareholders. An audit ensures that the financial management of the business is honest and professional. The audit protects the owners against misfeasance (unintentional violation of the law) or malfeasance (deliberate violation of the law) by employees who work with the finances for the business.

A CPA, therefore, can provide advice about a variety of financial matters, such as loans and the issuance of stock. It is useful to receive advice also on tax planning, mergers and acquisitions, financial strategies, and related matters.

Banker

Many new entrepreneurs mistakenly think that a banker is an antagonist whom they must overcome to get a loan. A banker, however, serves a vital role in the financing of the organization. This professional can help you maintain a healthy financial outlook for your business. You need a banker who perceives the banker's role as a consultant and advisor. The banker should work to help your business succeed, knowing that your success will contribute to the success of the bank. The following points explain the importance of a banker to your new business.

Banking services

You should find a bank that provides the banking services you need for your business. These include checking accounts, loans, lease programs, credit cards, electronic fund transfers, and financial planning. Banks have become more competitive today, and the variety and quality of services vary greatly.

Financial advice

A banker can provide you with advice about starting your business and arranging financing. Usually, the banker will expect to see a business plan and will give you guidance on how to create and develop a plan if you don't have one. The banker can also advise you on the most reasonable method to use in obtaining finances for your business.

Loans

A major service of a bank is the provision of business loans. Typical loans are for equipment and working capital. For new and rapidly expanding businesses, a major problem is cash flow. If you offer a product or service, you must pay to provide it, but your customers might not pay you for 30 to 60 days. Nevertheless, your business must have the capital to operate during this lag time. To help you meet your cash flow needs, a bank should be willing to provide a line of credit for your business.

Insurance Agent

A key element of any successful business is risk management. This refers to a plan for avoiding loss of business assets or earning capability. An insurance agent can show you how to manage your business risks by having several types of insurance.

Liability insurance

This insurance protects you from lawsuits that might result from injuries to other people or their property. Depending on your type of business, this might include premises insurance, product liability, officers and directors insurance, professional liability, and completed operations. Some types of businesses will benefit from liability insurance that protects the individual and the business from lawsuits that might arise from errors, omissions, or advice given.

Property insurance

Your business will need this type of insurance for protection against damage or theft to facilities, equipment, office furniture, and vehicles.

Earnings insurance

Three types of insurance fall into this category. First, *business interruption* insurance pays for the loss of business from damage to the business or from circumstances beyond your control, such as the shutdown of a key supplier. Second, *bad-debt* insurance covers bad debts above a specified limit. Third, *business owner's* insurance protects a business from loss due to an owner's death or permanent disability and ensures that the business will have the financial resources to continue in operation.

Fidelity bonds

A fidelity bond protects your business against employee theft. The government might require that you have a fidelity bond to do business with the government. A fidelity bond might also be required by some businesses, such as a cleaning service, to protect customers against theft.

Workers' compensation

Many states require that a business with employees carry workers' compensation insurance. This insurance pays for medical costs, rehabilitation costs, and reimbursement for lost wages to workers who are injured on the job. Usually, employers who carry workers' compensation insurance are protected from being sued for injuries. State laws on workers' compensation vary, so you will need advice from an insurance agent to determine the coverage needed for your business.

Life, health, and disability insurance

Business owners will need for themselves or their families these types of insurance to protect against personal loss. You might also want to provide these types of insurance for employees so that you can be competitive when hiring. A good insurance agent can advise you about which types of insurance are needed by your business. The agent can also recommend the coverage and deductible amounts that are most appropriate for your business.

Consultants

Consultants can often help a new business. You should seek the assistance of a consultant when you or your partners lack expertise in areas critical to the success of your business. Consultants offer services in a variety of areas such as those listed below.

Business start-up

Some consultants specialize in starting new businesses. They can help you develop your business plan, get financing, and identify a location for the business. Before you enlist the services of such consultants, make certain that their expertise exceeds that of consulting services available through community and government resources.

Management

A person with technical expertise might need help from a consultant who can provide general management advice.

Human resources/Training

Personnel management is subject to many laws and technicalities. If you hire employees, you might need the services of a consultant who can advise you on the development and management of personnel systems. If your employees need training, you might want to hire a professional trainer to conduct training sessions for you.

Technical expertise

You may need to hire a consultant who has technical expertise in the creation of a product or service that is integral to the operation of your company.

Consultants in the field

A valuable resource will be people who have gone into business for themselves and are working in the field or industry that interests you. They might have helpful advice on resources and opportunities, as well as suggestions about pitfalls to avoid.

Selection of Your Business Team

The professionals who become part of your business team are important to the success of your business. Through their work, they can make significant contributions to the growth of your business. A failure or mistake in their work, however, may have an adverse effect on your business. For this reason, you must select carefully each professional on the team. This section contains several useful guidelines for choosing professionals for your business team.

Identifying Professionals

You can identify professionals for your business a number of ways, but you should recognize that there is no substitute for time. The more time and effort that you expend in identifying professionals for your business team, the greater will be the likelihood of getting the right people.

To develop a list of professionals, first think of the professionals you already know. Then talk with friends, relatives, and business acquaintances about professionals they have used. Learn what experiences your contacts have had with these professionals and ask for opinions about their capabilities. You also should contact local professional associations and ask for referrals to professionals who are familiar with entrepreneurial enterprises.

After you have a list of names, don't be afraid to contact the professionals directly. Interview more than one in each specialty before making your selection. Talk to clients whom the professionals list as references. To determine which candidates are best for your business team, you might use the following criteria.

Competence of the individual

Professionals should be competent in their area of expertise. You can determine their competence in several ways. (1) Talk with a professional's clients and discuss their experiences with the person. (2) Ask them to describe the individual's strengths and weaknesses and give examples for each. (3) Interview the professional and ask for examples of experiences gained through working with a business like yours. (4) Compare professionals by contacting more than one. Don't settle for the first professional you contact in an area. Compare the responses they give to your questions and determine who appears to have the most expertise.

Comfort level

It is important that you feel comfortable working with the individual. You may spend a significant amount of time with this person whose advice may be important for the success of your business. The professional might have a great deal of expertise, but if you don't feel at ease with the person, you are less likely to seek this person's advice.

Care and attention

You need to be assured that the professional has the time and willingness to work with your business. A professional may be the best person in a particular field, and you may like the individual. If, however, the person is too busy or gives higher priority to other clients, you should look for someone else. You can often find professionals who are just starting their own business and will give your business extra care and attention. If the individual spends time researching what is best for your business, this effort often makes up for a lack of expertise.

Character

The professional you select must be trustworthy, honest, and reliable. No, the individual doesn't need to be a Girl Scout or Boy Scout! These traits, though, are necessary if you want to have a beneficial relationship. The professional must place the interests of your business above personal interests, or at least maintain a balance between them. The individual must recognize that personal success and the success of your business are interrelated. Furthermore, you need to be able to rely on this person's advice without having to do research to verify it.

Charges or fees

You must consider the professional's fees for services, when applicable. The amount of the fee, though, should be the least important of all the other factors you use in selecting a professional. A large fee doesn't ensure that the person is the best professional, nor does a low fee mean that the individual is inferior and uninformed. Ask for an explanation of the fee and why it differs from that of other professionals.

Selecting the Professional

While you reflect on which professional you should select to help your business, consider the following points:

1. How much experience with small businesses does the person have?

2. Does the person appear enthusiastic about working with your business?

3. Did the professional offer advice you found useful?

4. Are the references from other clients positive?

5. Can you afford the fees the professional will charge?

6. Can the professional provide the services you might need as your business grows?

7. Will the person continue to assist your business?

When you have considered these questions, make a T-chart for the professional, listing the individual's strengths on one side and weaknesses on the opposite side. This will help you decide which professional to select.

Strengths	Weaknesses

Professional Identification Exercise

This exercise helps you identify professionals who could become a part of your business team.

1. List the names of attorneys you know who might assist your business.

   _____

   _____

   _____

2. List the names of friends who could help you identify a good attorney for your business.

   _____

   _____

   _____

3. List the names of accountants you know who might assist your business.

   _____

   _____

   _____

4. List the names of friends who could help you identify a good accountant for your business.

_____

_____

_____

5. List the names of bankers you know who might assist your business.

_____

_____

_____

6. List the names of friends who could help you identify a good banker for your business.

_____

_____

_____

7. List the names of insurance agents you know who might assist your business.

_____

_____

_____

8. List the names of friends who could help you identify a good insurance agent for your business.

_____

_____

_____

9. What components of your business would benefit from the advice of a consultant? List each component and state the reason for seeking a consultant's help.

_____

_____

_____

10. List the names of consultants you know who might assist with your business.

_____

_____

_____

11. List the names of friends who could help you identify consultants for your business.

_____

_____

_____

12. List the names of individuals you know (or have been referred to) who have started or purchased a similar type of business. Who could you contact who has experience with what you hope to do?

_____

_____

_____

Summary

Assembling a competent, reliable, and enthusiastic business team is important for your new business. Members of this team can provide you with the legal, financial, and technical assistance that you need to build a successful business. The fees that you pay for this team of professionals will be a small investment compared to the benefits they will bring to your business. You should therefore select your business team carefully.

Endnote

1. Bradford W. Ketchum, Jr., "You and Your Attorney," *INC.* (June 1982), pp. 51-56.

Chapter 8
Beginning Operations

Every new business needs a facility in which to operate and a system for keeping records. The facility may be a room in your home, an office or suite you rent, or a building you lease or purchase. The records should include financial records, personnel records, and customer data.

Establishing an Office

To choose a facility, you need to consider its location, the type of facility that is best for your business, and the purchase of office equipment and supplies.

Choosing a Location

The first step in selecting a facility is to determine the best location for it. The following factors need to be considered.

Customers

A primary consideration is the location of your customers. Will they come often to your facility? If they will, you need to consider ease of access, parking, ground floor access, and visibility. Will you be manufacturing a product and shipping it to customers? If so, you need to consider ease of shipment to customers. Will you often go to your customers' locations? If that is true, you should consider the selection of a site near most of your customers.

For the business you might start, what issues do you need to consider in serving your customers?

_____

_____

Work force

A business that will require a significant number of employees should be located near a work force of a large number of people who possess the skills that will be needed for your business. You will also want to consider locating near education resources that can provide continued training to keep the skills of your work force current.

What kind of workers will your business need?

_____

_____

Preferences

Where would you enjoy working? You should consider your personal preferences as well as those of other principals in the business. You might prefer a location close to your home. You might want to move to a new part of the country. You might prefer a rural, urban, suburban, or metropolitan area.

What personal preferences do you have in selecting a location for your business?

_____

_____

Services

A business should be near the services and products that are necessary for its operation. Are there adequate utility supplies? Are there good telecommunication services available? Are there required suppliers nearby? Do you have access to support services such as consultants, marketing firms, print shops, and temporary personnel agencies?

What types of services will your business need?

_____

_____

Costs

You must keep in mind the expenses for a particular location. What is the average pay and type of fringe benefits expected by the work force in the area? What types of taxes must be paid? What are the costs of utilities? What will it cost to lease or buy a building? The costs for a location will affect the price of your product or service and the need for working capital.

Choosing a Facility

Once you have identified a location, you must select the facility. For this decision, you must determine the type of facility that will be most adequate for you. In selecting a facility, consider the following factors:

Number of employees needed

You should try to project the number of employees that your business will need in the next two to three years. This will help you determine the total amount of space, the number and size of rest rooms, the number of parking places, and the square footage of office or production space for each employee.

Customer access and service

There should be adequate parking space for customers. They should be able to access your building easily from the parking area. Drive-through services are important to many people who are busy. Likewise, your ability to deliver services to customers can be important.

Storage space

Make a list of all the equipment, inventory, and supplies that will need to be stored. Determine the method for storage and how much space this will require.

Production space

Unless you have a great deal of experience in the type of production done by your business, you will probably need an expert to help you calculate the production space that is required.

Office space

The amount and type of office space needed will depend on the total number of employees who will need office space, and the amount of privacy they will require. Once you consider these two concerns, you can calculate the amount of open space and private offices that will be needed. Unless privacy is a major concern, you are often better prepared for changes and growth in a new business when you plan for open office space.

Shipment processing and distribution

If you will be marketing products, you will need adequate space for packaging them. You will also require space to store the products until they are shipped.

Utilities

You will need access to utilities. These may include water, electricity, and gas. Furthermore, you will need to be sure that the electrical wiring is adequate for all machinery and office equipment.

You have three basic options for a facility for your business. The advantages and disadvantages of each are considered in the following paragraphs.

Working at home

Working at home is one inexpensive solution for a new business. American business is replete with legends of organizations that began in the owner's garage.

Advantages

1. Operating a business from your home is inexpensive.

2. Working at home is convenient compared to commuting to an office.

3. Working near your home can be relaxing compared to the stress of commuting.

4. Your work schedule at home can be flexible to fit your family's schedule.

5. By working at home, you might involve your family in the business.

Disadvantages

1. There can be many distractions at home, including children, visits from friends, and nonbusiness phone calls.

2. If you work by yourself at home, you may develop a feeling of isolation. This can be overcome by scheduling business luncheons and meetings with customers outside your home.

3. Some customers may perceive as unreliable and unprofessional a business that is run at home.

4. The danger of merging work and social life is greater at home. People who are workaholics are particularly vulnerable to this danger.

5. Your area may have zoning limitations that prevent working at home.

Renting an office or suite

An alternative to working at home is to rent or lease a single office or an office suite. It is often possible to find an executive suite where a receptionist, secretarial staff, and specialized office equipment can be shared with other professionals.

Advantages

1. Renting an office or suite can be relatively inexpensive.

2. An executive suite provides close associations with other professionals and might help you identify your business team.

3. You improve your image and, for a moderate cost, have many of the amenities of a larger business.

4. Usually, only a short-term commitment is required.

5. You can expand to other offices when available.

Disadvantages

1. You lose some control over the operation of your business and must use the personnel supplied by the executive suite management.

2. You are subject to the stability of the management. If the management company closes, you are out of office space and must relocate.

3. Competitors may be located in the same office suite.

4. You can use this option only when you have limited customer-access needs for a service-related business. You cannot use this option for production or inventory storage.

Leasing or purchasing a building

Another alternative is to lease or purchase a building when more than one person works in your business or when it has operations that are too large for an office environment.

Advantages

1. You have a great deal of control over the use and management of the facilities.

2. You have greater flexibility in being able to remodel the facilities as needed.

3. You will probably have greater parking availability and can control the use of parking at the facility.

4. The business might be able to expand if parts of the building aren't used at first or if you can expand the facility.

Disadvantages

1. Leasing or purchasing a building is the most expensive option.

2. You must purchase all of the furniture and equipment needed to run the operation.

3. You are responsible for maintenance if you purchase the facility.

4. If the business outgrows the space and there is no room for expansion, a mortgage or lease often limits your flexibility to move to another location.

What other advantages and disadvantages apply to each type of facility?

_____

_____

Which type of facility would be most appropriate for your business?

_____

_____

What specific advantages and disadvantages would apply in your situation?

Advantages	Disadvantages
_____	_____
_____	_____
_____	_____
_____	_____
_____	_____

Setting Up an Office

This section serves as a reminder about the basic equipment and supplies you need for setting up an efficient office.

Purchasing Equipment

You will need equipment to outfit an office for your business. General equipment includes furniture, a phone system, a computer system, and various office machines.

Furniture

The amount and type of furniture you will need depend on the type of business. If many customers come to your office, you will want to purchase high-quality furniture. If most customers won't see your office, furniture quality is less important. When you purchase furniture, think of functionality.

You can use following checklist to determine the furniture for your office. Check the items you will need to purchase.

_____ Desk	_____ Credenza
_____ Desk chair	_____ Side chairs
_____ File cabinet	_____ Bookcase
_____ Safe	_____ Work table
_____ Coat tree	_____ Sofa
_____ Easy chair	_____ Stereo system
_____ Storage cabinet	_____ Computer desk
_____ Lamp	_____ Side table

Phone system

Your phone system will be one of your most important tools because it will enable you to have good communication with customers. You would be well advised to hire a telecommunications consultant for one day to identify the most effective phone system for your business and to recommend the best vendors to supply the system.

The following is a list of items that you need to consider when installing a phone system. Estimate the number of lines and phones you will need for your business. Check the phone options that will be important for the operation of your business.

_____ Number of lines	_____ Number of phones
_____ 800 toll-free line	_____ Conferencing
_____ Paging	_____ Intercom
_____ Call forwarding	_____ Speaker phone
_____ Camp on	_____ Speed dialing
_____ Memory dialing	_____ Voice messaging

Computer system

A computer system can help you make effective use of modern office tools. The three software applications that you will most likely need are word processing, an electronic spreadsheet, and a database. If you plan to make presentations to customers, you should also purchase a presentation graphics program. Many computer systems are on the market, but buy one that you know is compatible with most of your customers' computer systems. System compatibility allows an easy exchange of data and information with your customers.

The following are items you might want to consider as a part of your computer system. Check the items that will be necessary for your business.

_____ Computer	_____ Portable computer
_____ Laser printer	_____ Modem
_____ Scanner	_____ Dot-matrix printer
_____ Fax board	_____ Tape backup
_____ Plotter	

Copier

A copier is essential to most businesses. You will need to make copies of financial records, proposals to customers, letters, and many other kinds of documents.

The following is a list of copier features you need to keep in mind during the selection process. Check the issues or features that are most important to you.

_____ Copies/minute	_____ Volume
_____ Sizing	_____ Color
_____ Paper size	_____ Cassettes
_____ Feeder	_____ Collator

Fax

A fax machine allows you to transmit images from one location to another. You must either have a dedicated phone line for the fax or buy a fax that senses when a fax message is incoming and switches from phone operation to fax operation. It is possible to install a fax or modem/fax board in your computer. This will allow you to transmit data to a fax machine or similarly equipped computer. This option, however, limits you to transmitting documents created with the computer unless you have a scanner.

Dictation unit

Having a portable dictation unit is helpful for making notes to yourself or for dictating documents. This unit will be particularly useful if you do much traveling.

Postage meter

A business that mails a large volume of letters or packages through the U.S. Postal Service will find a postage meter quite useful.

Purchasing Supplies

The best way to purchase office supplies is to get an office supply store catalog and go through it, making a list of the supplies you will need. You should consider also some special supplies.

Printed materials

You will want to have some special items printed. These should look attractive and project a professional image.

The following is a list of the printed items you might need. Check those that you think will be applicable for your business.

_____ Letterhead	_____ Envelopes
_____ Shipping envelopes	_____ Mailing labels
_____ Invoices	_____ Purchase orders
_____ Business cards	_____ Presentatiom folders

Time-appointment system

An entrepreneur should manage time effectively. For this, you may need an appointment and time management system. Many systems are available, so talk with friends and sales representatives to discover which one might work best for you.

Keeping Records

An important task in starting a business is to develop a system for record keeping which will ensure that all important data is retained in a well-organized manner. Some legal requirements exist for record keeping, so you should make certain that you are aware of them. A personal computer provides inexpensive but highly effective ways to store, organize, and retrieve records. This section reviews items that you need to consider in record keeping.

Financial Records

Many states require that a corporation use a double-entry bookkeeping system. If your business will be a proprietorship or partnership, you should consult with an accountant to determine the best bookkeeping system for your needs. An accountant can also advise you about whether to choose the cash method of accounting or the accrual method.

The following list contains financial records you should consider keeping. Check those that you feel you will use in your business.

_____ General ledger	_____ General journal
_____ Accounts receivable*	_____ Accounts payable*
_____ Payroll*	_____ Depreciation records*
_____ Cash receipts*	_____ Cash payments*
_____ Inventory*	_____ Sales*
_____ Payroll tax forms	

Those items marked with an asterisk (*) are required by law for tax purposes. An audit conducted by the IRS will expect you to provide data about these items. The use of checks, receipt books, sales slips, and payroll will help you meet these requirements.

Personnel Records

You must keep accurate and complete records about any employees you hire. Federal and state governments have many laws and regulations you must meet in the hiring, promotion, and termination of employees.

The following checklist will help you become aware of all of the forms you may need to keep for each employee. Check those forms that will apply to your business.

_____ Application	_____ Proof of citizenship
_____ I-9 form	_____ Withholding forms
_____ Copy of professional license	_____ Appraisals
_____ Disciplinary actions	_____ W-4 form

Customer Data

Customers are one of the most important assets your business will possess. You should retain information about your customers. If this information is complete and well organized, your business will be more valuable to a prospective buyer of your business.

The following list contains categories of customer information that might be recorded. Check the information that will be useful to your business.

_____ Customer name	_____ Address
_____ Phone number	_____ Contact
_____ Date of sales	_____ Sales amount
_____ Total sales	_____ Special needs

This section has indicated the types of records you must retain for your business. These records represent the minimum of record keeping for any organization. You will find that many other records are useful, such as those about suppliers, professional contacts, advertisers, consultants, and competitors' products.

Summary

The most important point to remember about starting a business operation is that it requires thorough planning. This chapter was designed to help you think about those aspects of operation that are common to most businesses. The location, facility, equipment, and records of the business are standard with all businesses. However, you will need to prepare your own checklist for items that have not been covered because they are specific to your business.

Chapter 9
Starting Your Own Consulting Firm

A chapter on consulting may seem unusual in a book on starting your own business, but consulting is itself a business that many professionals find attractive. You can become a consultant for a low investment, find that the market for good consultants is profitable, and learn that consulting offers a challenging career opportunity. There are strong indications of solid growth in the business opportunities for independent consultants.[1]

What Is Consulting?

Consulting is the provision of expert advice and services to an organization for improved performance within that organization. People become consultants for a variety of reasons, and consulting can take a number of forms. This chapter examines the motivations for consulting and the forms it can take.

Myths about Consulting

Dispelling some of the myths about consulting can help you determine whether it is the right career for you.

Consulting is glamorous

Most people who regard consulting as a glamorous career have viewed it from the outside. They see the opportunity, challenge, and flexibility that consulting offers, but they don't see the stress, time demands, and hard work that are required. Consulting can be extremely hard work, but it can provide a great deal of satisfaction.

It's great to be able to travel

Consultants often must travel across the country and sometimes to other countries. All of this travel may appear exciting, but it can become tiresome, frustrating, and lonely, particularly when a person is often away from family and friends. Despite these disadvantages, you do get to see interesting places and may have some flexibility in the amount of time that you travel.

Consultants have no ultimate responsibility

Many people who have dealt with consultants perceive their work to end with the report and recommendations they give to their clients. It appears that consultants don't have to live with their recommendations. Sometimes this is true, but the most effective consultants continue to work with their clients while recommendations are implemented and accept ultimate responsibility for their success or failure. Consultants who don't experience such success will not be used by a business again and will not be able to use the business for a reference.

As a consultant, you are your own boss

A consultant must walk a fine line in balancing client demands with personal interests. A consultant must be responsive to a client's needs. Occasionally, this may mean missing a family event or some other social activity in order to assist the client. Sometimes a client may expect or even demand that the consultant perform in accordance with some preset plan. When a client's expectations or demands become unreasonable, the consultant can explain to the client the limits of personal flexibility and even terminate a project when it seems impossible to work effectively with the client.

Kinds of Consulting

A person thinking about becoming a consultant often considers being an independent consultant, but several kinds of consulting should be considered. Each kind may or may not fit well into a specific legal structure. The kind of consulting you choose may therefore affect your choice of a legal structure for your business.

Part-time

You may want to consult part-time. This allows you to get a job with steady income but a flexible schedule that enables you to find time for consulting. You will need, however, to guard against possible conflicts of interest. A disadvantage is that you may not be able to meet many of a client's needs because of your job's demands.

Independent

An independent consultant is one who works alone. Some advantages of this form of consulting are low overhead and minimal management requirements. A disadvantage is that it is difficult for an independent consultant to do an extensive project for a client.

Networks

Many independent consultants who cannot conduct extensive projects for a client offset this limitation by developing a network of consultants who can be called in to assist with large projects. A disadvantage of this arrangement is that you must depend on the availability of the consultants in your network. They will, of course, give their own clients top priority.

Multiple staff

The advantages of developing a consulting firm with partners or hiring other consultants are that you can accept extensive contracts and develop a wide range of expertise among members of the firm. These advantages, however, are offset by the difficulty and stress of soliciting client projects to keep the staff employed. A multiple staff also requires that more time be spent in management. The result is that less time can be devoted to consulting.

Why Organizations Hire Consultants

The role a consultant performs when working with a client depends to a large extent on the expectations of the client. Organizations hire consultants for a number of reasons. You need to be aware of the hidden as well as the obvious motivations of a client in retaining your services.

Then you will be able to determine how effective you can be in meeting the client's needs and decide whether you want to accept the project.

Expert advice

The most straightforward reason to seek a consultant is that a business requires the person's expertise. In this case, the client wants the consultant to be available whenever advice is needed. This allows a consultant to develop a long-term relationship and provides a foundation for future projects and steady income.

Change agent

Organizations that are experiencing difficulties with management, operations, customer relations, and employee relations need a consultant who can identify the problems, make recommendations, and assist in helping the organization make the needed changes.

Not enough personnel

An organization may hire a consultant if the firm does not have adequate personnel to complete a project. This kind of work may present some difficulties for the consultant. The business may demand that the consultant do the work of a full-time employee but without full-time compensation. The business may even demand so much time and effort that the consultant can't work with other clients.

Short-term project

A short-term project enlists the consultant's expertise for a specific purpose and length of time. Such a project often involves a contract that contains all the details about the work of the project.

Objectivity

Sometimes a consultant is retained to provide objectivity in evaluating and solving a problem. The client's employees may be aware of what needs to be done but may need confirmation. In other cases, the employees may be so close to the problem that they fail to see the solution. A consultant offers the distinct advantage of being objective.

Serious problem

A consultant may be called in by a client who is desperate and has no idea of how to solve a serious problem. This kind of work can be a difficult challenge for the consultant for two reasons. First, the situation may have developed to a point where a solution is impossible. Second, the business may be in danger of failing because of the problem, and the consultant may not be able to collect a fee.

Political needs
Consultants are sometimes used for political reasons in an organization. A consultant may be brought in to make recommendations that managers feel would create a negative working environment should they make the recommendations. A client may seek a consultant to put a stamp of approval on a decision that has already been made. Political motivation creates one of the most difficult situations in which a consultant must function.

Excess budget
A client may retain a consultant's services because the end of a budget year is near and there is excess money to spend. Usually, for this kind of work, the client retains the consultant to conduct a short project. The most difficult challenge which this presents is that the consultant must operate under severe time constraints.

Setting Fees

A major question that people have when they become consultants is what fee to charge. They also wonder how they should charge time to their clients. Closely related to fee amounts and methods of charging time is the issue of how to market consulting services. The following sections address these concerns.

Setting fees begins with a careful assessment of your needs and expectations. How much money do you, as a consultant, want to earn? What benefits do you need? How many hours do you plan to invest in your business?

There are many ways to establish your fees. One way is to set a specific fee for each project. Other ways are to price a project by the hour or to charge by the deliverables. In choosing a method, think of the trade-offs for each project. Consider whether a project may be a long-term assignment. Determine whether other benefits make it possible to offer a more competitive fee.

Basic Assumptions

The first step in establishing your fee is to understand the criteria that must be considered for setting fees.

Business expenses

Your fee must cover all of your operating expenses, including rent, phone, insurance, supplies, and personnel. It is necessary that you compile a budget which contains all of your business expenses for the year.

Salary and fringe benefits

The fee must cover your salary and fringe benefits. Set your salary at a reasonable yet comfortable level. Include those fringe benefits that you find necessary.

Profit

You are entitled to make a profit over and above your salary. You will need to be prepared, though, to reinvest this money in research and marketing time, equipment and materials for your business, and retirement funds. At the beginning of your work as a consultant, it may be best to consider your profit as your reinvestment fund.

In addition to your projected expenses, you will invest time in marketing, managing, and researching that will not be reimbursed by anyone. Many individuals use a formula which suggests that one-third of your time will not be billable but will be your own investment. You must figure this time into your equation as you determine how much money you want to earn and how many billable hours you have in your work week.

Market

You need to consider the number of competitors, their fees, and their competence. Your fee must be competitive.

Perceptions

What fees seem reasonable to clients? You can determine this by talking to potential clients and other consultants. Make sure that you don't set your fees too low. A low fee is often interpreted by potential clients as an indication that you lack competence.

Billable Hours

To set an hourly fee, you must know your billable hours. To determine your billable hours, you subtract nonbillable hours from your total work hours. There are 2,080 hours in a work year (260 days x 8 hrs./day), but some of these hours are nonbillable, such as the following:

Holidays	72 hrs.
Vacation	80 hrs.
Sick days	40 hrs.
Administration	260 hrs. (5 hrs. per week)
Marketing	260 hrs. (5 hrs. per week)
Personal development	80 hrs.
Total nonbillable hours	**792 hrs.**

To determine the number of billable hours, you need to deduct the nonbillable hours from the total work hours.

Work hours per year	2,080 hrs.
Nonbillable hours	792 hrs.
Total billable hours	**1,288 yrs. (round to 1,300)**

Knowing your billable hours, you are ready to calculate an hourly fee. There are a couple of ways to do this.

Rule-of-Three Formula

The simplest method for calculating your fee is to use the *rule of three*. This rule derives its name from the fact that three components are used in calculating the amount of projected annual revenue that will be needed to function successfully.

Salary of consultant	1/3
Overhead + Benefits	1/3
Profit	1/3
Hourly fee =	**Projected annual revenue**
	÷ Yearly billable hours

Example:

Salary	$ 50,000
Overhead + Benefits	$ 50,000
Profit	$ 50,000
Projected annual revenue	**$150,000**

Hourly fee = **$150,000 ÷ 1,300 hrs.**

= $115.38 (round to $115)

Exact-Cost Method

The *exact-cost method* is the most pragmatic for consultants who have an unusual amount of overhead expenses. It is also more realistic, given the rising costs for all types of fringe benefits. It is not unusual for fringe benefits to amount to one-third of a person's salary. The formula for the exact-cost method is as follows:

Hourly fee =	Salary
+	Benefits
+	Expenses
+	Profit
÷	Yearly billable hours

Example:

Salary	$ 63,000
Benefits	$ 19,690
Expenses	$ 52,310
Profit	$ 35,000
Total	**$170,000**

Hourly fee = **$170,000 ÷ 1,300 hrs.**

= $130.77 (round to $131)

Fee Modification

Fees, like prices for all products and services, may be modified for a variety of reasons.

Industry standard

Your client's industry may have a standard fee that you must be willing to accept in order to do business with the client.

Competition

If you are familiar with fees of other consultants and feel that you must reduce your fee to compete, you should modify it.

Client perceptions

Clients who are not experienced in working with consultants may be surprised at your fee and expect you to lower it. Likewise, an experienced client may expect your fee to be similar to that of other consultants.

Size of contract

The larger a contract (in duration and the amount of work that you will do), the more you can consider lowering your fee to get the client's business. You can lower the cost because your marketing costs will be lower and the client may be willing to absorb normal operating expenses.

Length of relationship

You might consider a lower fee for a client who will be with you for a long time. The fee can be lower because of the savings in marketing expenses.

Obtain client's business

It may be wise to reduce your fee when you first begin working with a new client. This allows you to establish a relationship with the client. Later, after you have built a good reputation, you can announce that you need to increase your fee. The risk is the loss of a client, but a fee raise usually has a minimal effect when your work is highly valued.

Fee Arrangements

Consultants must have a plan for how they will charge clients for work performed. The fee arrangement should be convenient for the client but also protect your interests and investment of time. There are several possible fee arrangements.

Methods of Charging for Time

It is important that you develop a policy for charging your clients for the time that you perform work for them. You can choose from a number of options.

Hourly charge

One method is to bill for all hours that you actually work in completing a project. An hourly method is fair to a client because the client pays for only the actual time worked.

Daily charge

Another method is to level a daily charge regardless of the number of hours worked. Many consultants feel that this is a fair method to use because they must often set aside an entire day to work with a client regardless of the number of hours worked.

Fixed fee

A third method is to establish a set fee for the project you will conduct for a client. Some clients prefer this method, particularly if they fear an hourly or daily fee because they are not sure how much time a project will take and may think you will work longer than necessary. This method may prove disadvantageous to you, however, if you don't have experience in performing a project exactly like the one you will do for your client or if you haven't carefully assessed how long it will take to complete the project. The project may take much longer than you estimated.

Maximum fee (bracket)

A bracket fee protects both the consultant and the client. With this method, the consultant can use a high estimate for the amount of time required to complete a project. However, the client will be billed only for the actual amount of time needed to complete the project.

Retainer fee

A client may pay a retainer fee to guarantee that the services of a consultant will be available when they are needed. The consultant credits the retainer whenever work is done and informs the client about the amount of money remaining in the retainer fund.

Bonus fee

Some clients build in a bonus fee for the work consultants conduct for the clients. In some industries, bonus fees and percentage fees are considered unprofessional. In some instances, however, a bonus fee may be appropriate. Consultants who conduct projects that save a business money because of their timely efforts might expect a bonus when the completed work meets the clients' objectives.

Percentage fee

A percentage fee is a charge based on the amount of money that a consultant saves a business. For example, a consultant may agree to review utility usage by a business and then accept as a fee a percentage of the resultant savings.

Equity fee

A consultant may be willing to waive a fee in return for a percent of equity in a business. This arrangement can be useful to a business that is new and lacks the funds needed to retain the services of the consultant. This method also is used by consultants who specialize in business turnarounds.

A consultant might combine any of these methods for charging clients. The most important consideration is to be fair to both yourself and your clients.

Time to
Charge Clients

It is important that your clients understand clearly the ways in which you will charge for your time. The following list provides you with some basic guidelines related to appropriate charges.

Site visits

You should charge the client for any time that you spend at the client's place of business.

Research

Your client's project may require specialized research. Charging the client for such research is appropriate. Sometimes, however, you may do general research for information that you will use with other clients. For this kind of research, you should prorate your time to the estimated number of clients who you believe will use this information.

Project development

A client may expect you to prepare a detailed description of the project you will conduct. It is sometimes reasonable to expect the client to pay for this activity. This is particularly true when the plan could be used by an employee of the client to complete the project. You might want to tell the client that you will waive this fee if your plan is approved and your services are retained to carry out the plan.

Travel

Payment for time traveling to and from a client's place of business is reasonable. Most clients will be willing to pay for this time. However, it is common to charge only 50% of your fee for this time. This reduction can be justified by the fact that you can conduct other business and do some personal business while traveling.

Meetings/Conferences

You may need to attend a meeting, trade show, or conference to get information for your client. You should determine how specific the information must be for your client and whether you can use it for other clients. Let the client know exactly how much time you will bill in advance of your attendance. This arrangement will prevent misunderstanding.

Project costs

You should charge to your client all expenses directly related to a project. These charges should be specified and estimated as a part of the project's cost. Such charges include travel expenses and telephone calls.

Collecting Fees

An important aspect of managing a consulting firm is the collection of fees from clients. The failure to collect fees may result in the ultimate failure of your consulting business. This section examines why clients do not pay fees and how you can avoid this problem.

Reasons Clients Fail to Pay Consultant Fees

To collect your consulting fees, you should understand why some clients fail to pay for work that consultants perform.

No perceived worth

Information and expertise are nebulous commodities. When you provide them to clients, they might not perceive value in what you have done. For this reason, try to document your work with reports, project reviews, and computer databases.

Disagreement

A disagreement may arise between you and the client. The client must realize, however, that you must be paid regardless of a disagreement. You can convey this information by having a contract or letter of agreement that describes the project and specifies what recourse will be taken if there is a disagreement in the development of the project.

Misunderstanding of charges

Informing your clients in advance about your billing policies will prevent misunderstanding of your charges. Specify on your invoice why you are billing time. You might include with each invoice a progress report that provides more detail about the value of your services.

Variance from agreement

You should never do work that is not specified in your agreement with the client unless you have been given approval.

Perceived excess

A client may be reluctant to pay your bill because the time taken to complete an activity is perceived as excessive. Anticipate those situations and carefully document the reasons that the amount of time was necessary. It also helps to discuss a situation in advance with the client so that the client is forewarned.

Size of bill

Because of cash flow, a client may have difficulty paying a large bill. For this reason, you may want to break your time for a project into a number of smaller invoices that are sent over the course of the entire project. In fact, you may want to provide in the project proposal a timetable for invoicing the client and correlate the invoices with the completion dates of major activities connected with the project.

Disputed charges

In some instances, the client may disagree with a charge for time or expense incurred in completing a project. When this happens, try to resolve the problem through a personal contact. There may be circumstances, however, in which it is better to accept a loss than to lose altogether the client's business.

Inability to pay

A client may simply be unable to pay because of financial difficulties. You need to decide whether to write off the loss, continue to bill the client until payment is made, or possibly become a legal creditor in a bankruptcy case.

Avoiding Defaults on Client Payments

You will not want to experience many defaults by clients on their payments. If you follow several guidelines developed by experienced consultants, you can greatly reduce the potential for client defaults.

State fees
Make sure that your fees are stated in writing, in the form of a proposal or simply a letter.

State methods for charges
Make sure that the client knows the situations and time for which the client will be billed.

Establish project outcomes
Throughout the course of the project, have tangible outcomes that the client can use to measure your progress. A progress report can serve this purpose.

Have a written agreement
Whenever possible, provide the client with a written project proposal. This doesn't need to be a formal contract.

Bill regularly
Monthly billing is preferable because this is traditional in business and the client will be familiar with the procedure.

Discuss unusual costs
Make sure that you discuss any unusual costs connected with the project before incurring these expenses. The client will usually not challenge such costs.

Check client's credit
Conduct a credit check on a client with whom you are not familiar. A credit bureau can detail the procedure and the costs that will be associated with a credit check. Avoid a client who has a poor credit record unless you are willing to negotiate a special arrangement for the payment of your fee.

Steps in Marketing Consulting Services

The marketing of consulting services requires methods that differ from those of selling a tangible product. Consulting services are complex and require a higher level of conceptualization by the potential client than many other services require. This means that consultants must use a sophisticated approach to marketing. In most cases, the method used to contact a new client will need to be followed up by face-to-face contact with the potential client in order to sell the service.

Many consultants have failed because of haphazard marketing. This section describes the steps you should take to reach the ultimate goal of selling your services to a client.

Develop Your Services

The first and most important step is to define and develop the services or products you will offer to clients. To tell a client that you are a human resource development consultant is not sufficient. Do you specialize in compensation and fringe-benefit planning? Are you skilled in selection and interview procedures? Do you have special knowledge of career-development systems? The point is that clients need to know exactly what you can do for them. A consulting business built on selling the time of a consultant is limited in market potential. You can increase sales volume only by increasing the hourly fee. Therefore, it is necessary to think in broader terms about what you can sell.

Broker other consultant services

By developing a network of consultants, you may be able to broker the services of another consultant. For example, you might assist a business in developing a new computer system and discover that the telecommunications system needs to be evaluated. By arranging for the business to use the services of another consultant, you can receive a commission on the project. A reasonable percentage of the project is 10-15%.

Develop off-the-shelf packages

The term off-the-shelf package refers to a system that is already developed but can be applied in a variety of organizations. This requires extensive documentation and detailed information about the way in which the system functions. An example would be a customer service program. Suppose that you developed a system which a business could use to promote good customer service, manage customer service, and encourage the active participation of all employees. You might be the one to sell the program to a business. You might even train the employees on how to implement your system. The amount of time that you would take to do the training is short compared to the implementation of the entire consulting project.

License your products
Off-the-shelf packages can be licensed, as products, to other consultants. You train them on how to use your system, and they sell it to clients. You might license the product to a consultant for a flat fee or for a percentage of each sale the consultant makes to a client.

Develop seminars
Sometimes you can make more money on a seminar in a shorter time than you can through consulting. You can conduct seminars by working with firms that specialize in selling seminars, making arrangements through continuing education departments at universities, or setting up seminars directly by your consulting firm.

Use a speakers' bureau
It is possible to use a speakers' bureau to sell your services as a speaker. To do this, you need to have expertise, be recognized and respected in your field, and be an excellent speaker.

Publish books and newsletters
By publishing books and newsletters, you create products that you can sell to clients, their employees, attendees at seminars, other consultants, and the general public. Desktop publishing software makes it possible to do this type of publishing at a low cost. Published materials are also good marketing tools because they increase your name recognition.

Publish audio tapes, video tapes, or software
Making a small investment in the production of audio tapes or video tapes containing information that you provide as a consultant, seminar leader, or speaker can prove quite lucrative. They have the same potential as books.

Position Your Services

As a second step, you should position your services in a way that distinguishes you from other consultants. This requires that you identify other consultants in your area and discover the services they are providing. Specialize in an area they have ignored. Develop a service whose quality is markedly higher than the services of your competitors. Concentrate on extensive customer services.

Identify Potential Clients

The third step is to identify potential clients for your services. You can use a number of methods to accomplish this. The following are a few methods you can try.

Networking

Networking is probably your greatest means of identifying potential clients. Contact friends, relatives, and professional acquaintances to identify people or organizations that can use your service. Become visible to many people.

Referrals

Make friends with other consultants and determine how you can assist them rather than compete against them. Share referrals with these consultants to expand your network. Ask clients for referrals to other businesses that might consider using your services.

Chambers of commerce

Many chambers of commerce will sell their mailing lists. It is possible to join a chamber of commerce for a small fee. Membership usually entitles you to a directory of the chamber members. Participation in chamber activities will increase your contacts and make members of the business community aware of your services.

Request-for-proposals (RFPs)

RFPs are published by government agencies, nonprofit organizations, and some businesses. These are announcements about the need for a service. Normally, the announcement will specify how you can obtain a copy of the RFP, which will detail the contents of the proposal that you must write in order to be considered for the contract. The *Commerce Business Daily* is published by the federal government and lists many RFP notices. Some state governments have a similar publication. Contact your state department of commerce or state purchasing agency to find out about such a publication. Watch for announcements in local newspapers. Some state and federal agencies will put you on a mailing list and send you notifications if you request this service.

Yellow Pages

Go through the *Yellow Pages* and identify potential businesses that would be interested in your services. Many areas have a blue book that lists the addresses and telephone numbers of businesses.

Mailing lists

You can purchase mailing lists that contain the names, addresses, and telephone numbers of businesses. These lists can be highly specialized and thus increase the chance that they will contain the names of businesses likely to retain your services.

Get the Message Out

After you identify potential customers, the fourth step is to make them aware of your services. Your goal is to entice a potential client into allowing you to make a visit. Try using some of the following methods to spread information about your services.

Speaking

Speak at civic groups, nonprofit associations, professional associations, business luncheons, and any other events that will put you in contact with other people.

Publications

Send out a newsletter to potential clients. The newsletter should demonstrate your knowledge and expertise in a particular area. The publication, however, should be a teaser in that it gives valuable information but leaves potential clients wanting to find out more. In one section of your newsletter, make clear the services you offer and how a business can contact you to obtain additional information.

Telemarketing

Prepare a 30-second sales pitch you can deliver over the phone. Be sure that you first identify the person who can make a decision about retaining your services.

Direct mail

Sending out large quantities of advertising through the mail is useful in getting your name in front of people. To be effective, the mailing must be followed up with a telephone call.

Advertising

You can contact potential clients through advertising. Direct the advertising to business owners and managers. Advertise in the business section of local newspapers. Identify publications that are directed toward the business market and advertise in these.

Sell Your Services

To sell your services, you will need to meet with a potential client. A repeat client, however, may be willing to purchase your services by phone or by receiving a written proposal. The following are tips for meetings whose purpose is to obtain a client's business.

Appearance

Always attend the meeting in a suit. This applies regardless of gender. People will be more impressed than when you dress casually.

Written material

At the meeting, have written material you can distribute to the potential client. The material may include a description of your services, fee structure, methods of operation, experience and education, and prior consulting projects.

Prepared presentation

Make a formal presentation. Use overhead transparencies, a small flip chart, or handouts that contain the basic information you need to convey to the prospective client. You should specify the services you have to offer, explain their benefits to the client's business, summarize your expertise, and ask the potential client to identify how you can specifically be of assistance. Gather as much information as you can about the client's needs and indicate how your services can meet those needs.

Formal proposal

You may need to follow up an initial contact by writing a formal proposal. This must be written according to the format required in an RFP if one is presented by the potential client. In those situations where you are not responding to an RFP, the following format will be effective in presenting your ideas to an organization's management:

1. Overview

2. Description of Organization

3. Statement of Need

4. Experience of Staff (who will work on the project)

5. Prior Experience with Organization

6. Work Plan

7. Benchmarks That Are Matched to Objectives

8. Schedule

9. Project Budget

10. Benefits to the Organization

11. Conclusion

If possible, read proposals that have been prepared by other consultants. Proposal writing is an art and improves through practice.

Remain in Contact with Your Client

Robert Kelley, an author on consulting, cites a survey by the Institute of Management Consultants, which indicates that 70% of the business done by consultants is from former clients, and 15% of the business is from referrals by former clients.[2] When a project is completed, talk with the client and make sure that the person is completely satisfied. Let the client know that you would like to do business with that individual again. Call about every three months just to visit with the client or to take the person to lunch. This may give you an opportunity to provide additional consulting services or to learn of another referral.

Consultant Assessment Exercise

For this exercise, consider each statement or question and present your response in the space provided.

1. List the advantages and disadvantages that relate to your interest in consulting.

   Advantages   **Disadvantages**

   _____   _____

   _____   _____

   _____   _____

   _____   _____

   _____   _____

   _____   _____

   _____   _____

   _____   _____

   _____   _____

2. What specific skills do you possess that you could market as a consultant?

   a. _____

   b. _____

   c. _____

   d. _____

   e. _____

   f. _____

   g. _____

3. Write a one-sentence description of a service you could provide as a consultant that would be highly valued by businesses in your area.

_____

_____

_____

_____

_____

_____

_____

4. What fee do you think a client would be willing to pay for this service?

_____

5. List other consultants in your area who provide the type of consulting service you would offer.

a. _____

b. _____

c. _____

d. _____

e. _____

f. _____

g. _____

6. Describe how you could position your consulting service to compete effectively against these consultants.

_____

_____

_____

_____

_____

_____

_____

_____

7. Indicate with a check mark how you assess your potential as a consultant.

___Excellent   ___Very Good   ___Good   ___Fair   ___Poor

Summary

Consulting provides an opportunity for professionals with a valuable set of skills or knowledge to start a business with a minimal amount of investment. You must approach the consulting business as you would any other. This means following the advice given in the preceding chapters. The major investment that you will make in starting a consulting firm is your time. With patience, hard work, and continued improvement, many business people can succeed in their own enterprises.

Endnotes

1. Herman Holtz, *How to Succeed as an Independent Consultant* (New York: John Wiley & Sons, Inc., 1988), p. xv.

2. Robert E. Kelley, Consulting: *The Complete Guide to a Profitable Career* (New York, Charles Scribner's Sons, 1986), p. 123.

SMALL BUSINESS ADMINISTRATION OFFICES

Type	City	State	Zip Code	Address	Phone Number
DO	Birmingham	AL	35203-2398	2121 8th Ave. N.	(205) 731-1344
DO	Anchorage	AK	99513	222 West 8th Avenue	(907) 271-4022
DO	Phoenix	AZ	85004	2828 N. Central Ave.	(602) 640-2316
POD	Tucson	AZ	85701	300 West Congress St.	(602) 670-4759
DO	Little Rock	AR	72202	2120 Riverfront Drive	(501) 324-5278
DO	San Francisco	CA	94105	71 Stevenson Street	(415) 744-6402
DO	Fresno	CA	93727	2719 N. Air Fresno Dr.	(209) 487-5189
DO	Glendale	CA	91203	330 N. Brand Blvd.	(213) 894-2956
DO	San Diego	CA	92188	880 Front Street	(619) 557-7252
DO	San Francisco	CA	94105	211 Main Street	(415) 744-6820
DO	Santa Ana	CA	92703	901 W. Civic Center Dr.	(714) 836-2494
BO	Sacramento	CA	95814	660 J Street	(916) 551-1426
POD	Ventura	CA	93003	6477 Telephone Road	(805) 642-1866
RO	Denver	CO	80202	999 18th Street	(303) 294-7021
DO	Denver	CO	80201	721 19th Street	(303) 844-3984
DO	Hartford	CT	06106	330 Main St.	(203) 240-4700
DO	Washington	DC	20036	1111 18th St., NW	(202) 634-1500
BO	Wilmington	DE	19801	920 N. King St.	(302) 573-6295
DO	Jacksonville	FL	32256-7504	7825 Baymeadows Way	(904) 443-1900
DO	Coral Gables	FL	33146-2911	1320 S. Dixie Hgwy.	(305) 536-5521
POD	Tampa	FL	33602-3945	501 E. Polk St.	(813) 228-2594
POD	W. Palm Beach	FL	33407-2044	5601 Corporate Way	(407) 689-3922
RO	Atlanta	GA	30367	1375 Peachtree St., NE	(404) 347-2797
DO	Atlanta	GA	30309	1720 Peachtree Rd., NW	(404) 347-4749
POD	Statesboro	GA	30458	52 N. Main St.	(912) 489-8719
DO	Honolulu	HI	96850	300 Ala Moana Blvd.	(808) 541-2990
DO	Boise	ID	83702	1020 Main Street	(208) 334-1096
RO	Chicago	IL	60606-6611	300 S. Riverside Plaza	(312) 353-5000
DO	Chicago	IL	60661-1093	500 W. Madison St.	(312) 353-4528
BO	Springfield	IL	62704	511 W. Capitol St.	(217) 492-4416
DO	Indianapolis	IN	46204-1873	429 N. Pennsylvania	(317) 226-7272
DO	Cedar Rapids	IA	52402	373 Collins Road, NE	(319) 393-8630
DO	Des Moines	IA	50309	210 Walnut Street	(515) 284-4422
DO	Wichita	KS	67202	100 East English St.	(316) 269-6273
DO	Louisville	KY	40202	600 Dr. M.L. King Jr Pl.	(502) 582-5976
DO	New Orleans	LA	70112	1661 Canal Street	(504) 589-2744
POD	Shreveport	LA	71101	500 Fannin Street	(318) 226-5196
DO	Augusta	ME	04330	40 Western Ave.	(207) 622-8378
DO	Baltimore	MD	21202	10 N. Calvert St.	(410) 962-4392
RO	Boston	MA	02110	155 Federal St.	(617) 451-2023
DO	Boston	MA	02222-1093	10 Causeway St.	(617) 565-5590
BO	Springfield	MA	01103	1550 Main St.	(413) 785-0268
DO	Detroit	MI	48226	477 Michigan Ave.	(313) 226-6075
BO	Marquette	MI	49885	300 S. Front St.	(906) 225-1108
DO	Minneapolis	MN	55403-1563	100 N. 6th St.	(612) 370-2324
RO	Kansas City	MO	64106	911 Walnut Street	(816) 426-3608
DO	Kansas City	MO	64105	323 West 8th Street	(816) 374-6708
DO	St. Louis	MO	63101	815 Olive Street	(314) 539-6600
BO	Springfield	MO	65802	620 S. Glenstone St.	(417) 864-7670
DO	Jackson	MS	39201	101 W. Capitol St.	(601) 965-5325
BO	Gulfport	MS	39501-7758	1 Hancock Plaza	(601) 863-4449
DO	Helena	MT	59626	301 South Park	(406) 449-5381

RO - Regional Office   DO - District Office   BO - Branch Office   POD - Post of Duty

Type	City	State	Zip Code	Address	Phone Number
DO	Omaha	NE	68154	11145 Mill Valley Rd.	(402) 221-3604
DO	Las Vegas	NV	89125	301 East Stewart St.	(702) 388-6611
POD	Reno	NV	89505	50 South Virginia St.	(702) 784-5268
DO	Concord	NH	03302-1257	143 N. Main St.	(603) 225-1400
DO	Newark	NJ	07102	60 Park Place	(201) 645-2434
POD	Camden	NJ	08104	2600 Mt. Ephrain Dr.	(609) 757-5183
DO	Albuquerque	NM	87104	625 Silver Avenue, SW	(505) 766-1870
RO	New York	NY	10278	26 Federal Plaza	(212) 264-1450
DO	Buffalo	NY	14202	111 West Huron St.	(716) 846-4301
DO	New York	NY	10278	26 Federal Plaza	(212) 264-2454
DO	Syracuse	NY	13260	100 S. Clinton St.	(315) 423-5383
BO	Elmira	NY	14901	333 East Water St.	(607) 734-8130
BO	Melville	NY	11747	35 Pinelawn Rd.	(516) 454-0750
BO	Rochester	NY	14614	100 State St.	(716) 263-6700
POD	Albany	NY	12207	445 Broadway	(518) 472-6300
DO	Charlotte	NC	28202	200 N. College St.	(704) 344-6563
DO	Fargo	ND	58102	657 2nd Ave North	(701) 239-5131
DO	Cleveland	OH	44199	1240 E. 9th St.	(216) 522-4180
DO	Columbus	OH	43215	85 Marconi Blvd.	(614) 469-6860
BO	Cincinnatti	OH	45202	525 Vine St.	(513) 684-2814
DO	Oklahoma City	OK	73102	200 North West 5th St.	(405) 231-4301
DO	Portland	OR	97201	222 S.W. Columbia	(503) 326-5223
RO	King Of Prussia	PA	19406	475 Allendale Rd.	(215) 962-3700
DO	King Of Prussia	PA	19406	475 Allendale Rd.	(215) 962-3804
DO	Pittsburgh	PA	15222	960 Penn Ave.	(412) 644-2780
BO	Harrisburg	PA	17101	100 Chestnut St.	(717) 782-3840
BO	Wilkes-Barre	PA	18702	20 N. Pennsylvania Ave.	(717) 826-6497
DO	Providence	RI	02903	380 Westminister Mall	(401) 528-4561
DO	Columbia	SC	29201	1835 Assembly St.	(803) 765-5376
DO	Sioux Falls	SD	57102	101 South Main Avenue	(605) 330-4231
DO	Nashville	TN	37228-1500	50 Vantage Way	(615) 736-5881
RO	Dallas	TX	75235	8625 King George Dr.	(214) 767-7635
DO	Dallas	TX	75242	1100 Commerce Street	(214) 767-0600
DO	El Paso	TX	79935	10737 Gateway West	(915) 541-5676
DO	Houston	TX	77054	2525 Murworth	(713) 660-4401
DO	Harlingen	TX	78550	222 East Van Buren St.	(512) 427-8533
DO	Lubbock	TX	79401	1611 Tenth Street	(806) 743-7462
DO	San Antonio	TX	78216	7400 Blanco Road	(512) 229-4535
BO	Corpus Chris	TX	78476	606 North Carancahua	(512) 888-3301
BO	Ft. Worth	TX	76102	819 Taylor Street	(817) 334-3777
POD	Austin	TX	78701	300 East 8th Street	(512) 482-5288
POD	Marshall	TX	75670	505 East Travis	(903) 935-5257
DO	Salt Lake City	UT	84138	125 South State St.	(801) 524-5800
DO	Montpelier	VT	05602	87 State St.	(802) 828-4422
DO	Richmond	VA	23240	400 N. 8th St.	(804) 771-2400
RO	Seattle	WA	98121	2615 4th Avenue	(206) 553-5676
DO	Seattle	WA	98174	915 Second Avenue	(206) 220-6520
DO	Spokane	WA	99204	West 601 First Ave.	(509) 353-2810
DO	Clarksburg	WV	26301	168 W. Main St.	(304) 623-5631
BO	Charleston	WV	25301	550 Eagan St.	(304) 347-5220
DO	Madison	WI	53703	212 E. Washington Ave.	(608) 264-5261
BO	Milwaukee	WI	53203	310 W. Wisconsin Ave.	(414) 297-3941
DO	Casper	WY	82602	100 East B Street	(307) 261-5761

RO - Regional Office   DO - District Office   BO - Branch Office   POD - Post of Duty

SMALL BUSINESS DEVELOPMENT CENTERS

ALABAMA

Alabama Small Business Development Center
Mr. John Sandefur, State Director
(205) 934-7260 FAX: (205) 934-7645
UNIVERSITY OF ALABAMA AT BIRMINGHAM
Medical Towers Building
1717 11th Avenue South, Suite 419
Birmingham, Alabama 35294

Alabama International Trade Center
Ms. Nisa Miranda, Director (205) 348-7621
University of Alabama
Box 870396 400-N, Martha Parham West
Tuscaloosa, Alabama 35487-0396

Alabama Small Business Procurement System
vacant (205) 934-7260
University of Alabama at Birmingham
Small Business Development Center
1717 11th Avenue South, Suite 419
Birmingham, Alabama 35294

Alabama State University
Ms. Jacqueline Gholston, Director (205) 269-1102
Small Business Development Center
915 South Jackson Street
Montgomery, Alabama 36195

Auburn University
Ms. Kim Kuerten, Director (205) 844-4220
Small Business Development Center
College of Business, 226 Thach Hall
Auburn, Alabama 36849-5243

Jacksonville State University
Mr. Pat W. Shaddix, Director (205) 782-5271
Small Business Development Center
113-B Merrill Hall
Jacksonville, Alabama 36265

Livingston University
Ms. Yolanda Devine, Director
(205) 652-9661
Small Business Development Center
Ext. 439, Station 35
Livingston, Alabama 35470

North East Alabama Regional
Mr. Jeff Thompson, Director (205) 535-2061
Small Business Development Center
P.O. Box 343, 225 Church Street, N.W.
Huntsville, Alabama 35804-0343

Troy State University
Ms. Janet Bradshaw, Director (205) 670-3771
Small Business Development Center
Sorrell College of Business
Troy, Alabama 36082-0001

University of Alabama
Mr. Paavo Hanninen, Director (205) 348-7011
Small Business Development Center
P.O. Box 870397, 400-S Martha Parham West
Tuscaloosa, Alabama 35487-0397

University of Alabama at Birmingham
Mr. Vernon Nabors, Director (205) 934-6760
Small Business Development Center
901 South 15th Street, MCJ, Room 143
Birmingham, Alabama 35294-2060

University of North Alabama
Dr. William S. Stewart, Director (205) 760-4629
Small Business Development Center
P.O. Box 5017, Keller Hall
Florence, Alabama 35632-0001

University of South Alabama
Ms. Cheryl Coleman, Director (205) 460-6004
Small Business Development Center
College of Business & Management Studies,
BMSB 101
Mobile, Alabama 36688

ARIZONA

Arizona Small Business Development Center
Mr. Dave Smith, State Director
(602) 392-5224 FAX: (602) 392-5300
GATEWAY COMMUNITY COLLEGE
108 North 40th Street, Suite 148
Phoenix, Arizona 85034

Arizona Western College
Mr. Richard Meyer, Director (602) 341-1650
Small Business Development Center
Century Plaza, 281 West 24th Street, #128
Yuma, Arizona 85364

Central Arizona College
Dr. Bill Phillips, Director (602) 723-5522
Small Business Development Center
Gila Career Center
P. O. Box 339
Sacaton, Arizona 85247

Cochise College
Mr. Phil Stickney, Director (602) 459-9778
Small Business Development Center
901 North Colombo, Room 411
Sierra Vista, Arizona 85635

Eastern Arizona College
Mr. Frank Granberg, Director (602) 428-7603
Small Business Development Center
1111 Thatcher Boulevard
Safford, Arizona 85546

Gateway Community College
Ms. Kathy Evans, Director (602) 392-5220
Small Business Development Center
3901 East Van Buren, #150
Phoenix, Arizona 85008

Mohave Community College
Ms. Dorene Jordan, Director (602) 453-1836
Small Business Development Center
1941 San Juan Drive
Lake Havasu City, Arizona 86403

Northland Pioneer College
Mr. Joel Eittreim, Director (602) 537-2976
Small Business Development Center
1001 Deuce of Clubs
Show Low, Arizona 85901

Pima Community College
Mr. John Gabusi, Acting Director
(602) 884-6306
Small Business Development Center
655 North Alvernon, #112
Tuscon, Arizona 85711

Rio Salado Community College
Ms. Patti Wilde, Director (602) 238-9603
Small Business Development Center
301 West Roosevelt, Suite D
Phoenix, Arizona 85003

Yavapai College
Mr. Richard Senopole, Director (602) 776-2374
Small Business Development Center
1100 East Sheldon Street
Prescott, Arizona 86301

ARKANSAS

Arkansas Small Business Development Center
Mr. Paul McGinnis, State Director
(501) 324-9043 FAX: (501) 324-9049
UNIVERSITY OF ARKANSAS AT LITTLE ROCK
Little Rock Technology Center Building
100 South Main, Suite 401
Little Rock, Arkansas 72201

Arkansas State University
Mr. Gerald Jones, Director (501) 972-3517
Small Business Development Center
P.O. Drawer 2650
Jonesboro, Arkansas 72467

Arkansas State University
Mr. David Money, Director (501) 882-6452
Beebe Branch
Small Business Development Center, Drawer H
Beebe, Arkansas 72012-1008

Harding University
Dr. Bob Reely, Director (501) 268-6161
Small Business Development Center
Mabee School of Business Building
Blakeny and Center Streets
Searcy, Arkansas 72143

Anderson State University
Mr. William Akin, Director (501) 246-5511
Small Business Development Center
1054 Huddleston, P.O. Box 2231
Arkadelphia, Arkansas 71923

University of Arkansas at Fayetteville
Dr. Don Cook, Director (501) 575-5148
Small Business Development Center
College of Business - BA 117
Fayetteville, Arkansas 72701

University of Central Arkansas
Dr. Homer Saunders, Director (501) 450-3190
Small Business Development Center
Burdick Business Administration Bldg.
Conway, Arkansas 72032

CALIFORNIA

California Small Business Development Center
Dr. Edward Kawahara, State Director
(916) 324-9234 FAX: (916) 322-3524
DEPARTMENT OF COMMERCE
Office of Small Business
1121 L Street, Suite 600
Sacramento, California 95814

Butte College Tri-Counties
Ms. Kay Zimmerlee, Manager (916) 895-9017
Small Business Development Center
260 Cohasset Avenue
Chici, California 95927

Central Coast
Mr. Mark Bleadon, Manager (408) 479-6136
Small Business Development Center
6500 Soquel Drive
Aptos, California 95003

East Bay
Ms. Selma Taylor, Manager (415) 893-4114
Small Business Development Center
2201 Broadway, Suite 814
Oakland, California 94612

Eastern Los Angeles
Ms. Toni Valdez, Manager (714) 629-2247
Small Business Development Center
363 South Park Avenue, Suite 105
Pomona, California 91766

Gavilan College
Mr. Peter Graff, Manager (408) 479-0373
Small Business Development Center
5055 Santa Teresa Boulevard
Gilroy, California 95020

Greater Sacramento
Ms. Debbie Travis, Manager (916) 920-7949
Small Business Devlopment Center
1787 Tribute Road, Suite A
Sacramento, California 95815

Greater San Diego Chamber of Commerce
Ms. Maria Morris, Manager (619) 463-9388
Small Business Development Center
4275 Executive Square, Suite 920
San Diego, California 92037

Inland Empire
Mr. Steve Pontell, Manager (714) 941-7877
Small Business Development Center
800 North Haven Avenue, Suite 100
Ontario, California 91764

Napa Valley College
vacant (707) 253-3210
Small Business Development Center
100 Combs Street
Napa, California 94559

North Coast
Ms. Fran Clark, Manager (707) 464-2168
Small Business Development Center
882 H Street
Crescent City, California 95531

Northern Los Angeles
Mr. John Rooney, Manager (818) 989-4377
Small Business Development Center
14540 Victory Boulevard, Suite 200
Van Nuys, California 91411

Orange County
Gregory F. Kishel, Director
Susan S. Fox, Business Management Consultant
(714) 647-1172 FAX: (714) 835-9008
Small Business Development Center
901 East Santa Ana Blvd., Suite 101
Santa Ana, California 92701

San Joaquin Delta College
Ms. Gillian Murphy, Manager (209) 474-5089
Small Business Development Center
5151 Pacific Avenue
Stockton, California 95207

Sierra College
Mr. Art Curry, Manager (916) 885-5488
Small Business Development Center
550 High Street, #3
Auburn, California 95603

Silicon Valley, San Mateo County
Mr. Gary Serda, Manager (408) 298-8455
Small Business Development Center
380 North First Street, Suite 202
San Jose, California 95112

Small Business Development Center of
Lake and Mendocino Counties
vacant (707) 263-0630
341 North Main Street
Lakeport, California 95453

Solano County
Mr. Edward Schlenker, Manager (707) 864-3382
Small Business Development Center
320 Campus Lane
Suisun, California 94585

Southern California Export Assistance
Mr. Fargo Wells, Manager (213) 749-8698
Small Busines Development Center
124 East Olympic Boulevard, Suite 517
Los Angeles, California 90015

Southwestern College
vacant (619) 421-2156
Small Business Development and
International Trade Center
900 Otay Lakes Road, Bldg. 1600
Chula Vista, California 91910

Valley Sierra
Mr. Kelly Bearden, Manager (209) 521-6177
Small Business Development Center
1012 Eleventh Street, Suite 210
Modesto, California 95354

Weill Institute
Mr. Jeffrey Johnson, Manager (805) 395-4148
Small Business Development Center
2101 K Street Mall
Bakersfield, California 93301

COLORADO

Colorado Small Business Development Center
Mr. Rick Garcia, State Director
(303) 892-3840 FAX: (303) 892-3848
OFFICE OF BUSINESS DEVELOPMENT
1625 Broadway, Suite 1710
Denver, Colorado 80202

Adams State College
Mr. Richard Turney, Director (719) 589-7372
Small Business Development Center
Alamosa, Colorado 81102

Arapahoe Community College
Ms. Selma Kristel, Director (303) 795-5855
Small Business Development Center
South Metro Denver Chamber of Commerce
1101 West Mineral Avenue, Suite 160
Littleton, Colorado 80120

Burlington City Hall
Mr. Larry O'Neill, Director (719) 346-9311
Small Business Development Center
480 15th Street
Burlington, Colorado 80807-1624

Colorado Mountain College
Mr. Jim Kraft, Director (303) 476-4040 1-800-621-1647
Small Business Development Center
1310 Westhaven Drive
Vail, Colorado 81657

Colorado Northwestern Community College
Mr. Ken Farmer, Acting Director (303) 824-7071
Small Business Development Center
50 Spruce Drive
Craig, Colorado 81625

Community College of Aurora
Ms. Kathy Scott, Director (303) 360-4745
Small Business Development Center
791 Chambers Road, #302
Aurora, Colorado 80011

Community College of Denver
Ms. Carolyn Love, Director (303) 620-8076
Small Business Development Center
1445 Market Street
Denver, Colorado 80202

Delta Montrose Vocational School
Mr. Larry Fay, Director (303) 874-7671
Small Business Development Center
1765 US Highway 50
Delta, Colorado 81416

Grand Junction Business Incubator
Mr. Bob Sikora, Director (303) 248-7314
Small Business Development Center
304 West Main Street
Grand Junction, Colorado 81505-1606

Greeley/Weld Chamber of Commerce
vacant (303) 352-3661
Small Business Development Center
1407 Eighth Avenue
Greeley, CO 80631

Fort Lewis College
Mr. Bard Heroy, Director (303) 247-7188
Small Business Development Center
Miller Student Center, Room 108
Durango, Colorado 81301

Front Range Community College
Mr. Michael Lenzini, Director (303) 466-8811
Small Business Development Center
3645 West 112th Avenue
Westminster, Colorado 80030

Lamar Community College
Mr. Elwood Gillis, Director (719) 336-8141
Small Business Development Center
2400 South Main
Lamar, Colorado 81052

Morgan Community College
Mr. Randy Johnson, Director (303) 867-3351
Small Business Development Center
300 Main Street
Fort Morgan, Colorado 80701

Pikes Peak Community College
Ms. Kathy Wallace, Director (719) 635-1551
Colorado Springs Chamber of Commerce
Small Business Development Center
102 Cascade Street, Sixth Floor
Colorado Springs, Colorado 80901

Pueblo Community College
vacant (719) 549-3224
Small Business Development Center
900 West Orman Avenue
Pueblo, Colorado 81004

Red Rocks Community College
Mr. Jeff Seifried, Director (303) 987-0710
Small Business Development Center
13300 West Sixth Avenue
Lakewood, Colorado 80401-5398

Trinidad State Junior College
Mr. Paul Cordova, Director (719) 846-5645
Small Business Development Center
600 Prospect Street, Davis Science Building
Trinidad, Colorado 81082

CONNECTICUT

Connecticut Small Business Development Center
Mr. John O'Connor, State Director
(203) 486-4135 FAX: (203) 486-1576
UNIVERSITY OF CONNECTICUT
School of Business Administration
368 Fairfield Road: Box U-41, Room 422
Storrs, Connecticut 06269-2041

Business Regional B.C.
Mr. Juan Scott, Director (203) 335-3800
Small Business Development Center
10 Middle Street, 14th Floor
Bridgeport, Connecticut 06604-429

Greater New Haven Chamber of Commerce
Mr. Neal Wehr, Director (203) 773-0782
Small Business Development Center
195 Church Street
New Haven, Connecticut 06506

Greater Waterbury Chamber of Commerce
Ms. Eileen Oppenheimer, Director (203) 757-0701
Small Business Development Center
83 Bank Street
Waterbury, Connecticut 06702

University of Bridgeport
Mr. Bernard I. Friedlander, Director (203) 576-4572
Small Business Development Center
141 Linden Avenue
Bridgeport, Connecticut 06601

University of Connecticut
Mr. William Lockwood, Director (203) 449-1188
Small Business Development Center
Administration Building, Room 313
1084 Shennecossett Road
Groton, Connecticut 06340-6097

University of Connecticut/MBA
Mr. Richard Rogers, Director (203) 241-4984
Community Accounting Aid and Services
Small Business Development Center
1800 Asylum Avenue
West Hartford, Connecticut 06117

DELAWARE

Delaware Small Business Development Center
Ms. Linda Fayerweather, State Director
(302) 451-2747 FAX: (302) 451-6750
UNIVERSITY OF DELAWARE
Purnell Hall - Suite 005
Newark, Delaware 19716

DISTRICT OF COLUMBIA

Metropolitan Washington Small Business
Ms. Nancy Flake, Director
(202) 806-1550 FAX: (202) 806-1777
Development Center
HOWARD UNIVERSITY
2600 Sixth Street, N.W.
Washington, D.C. 20059

Gallaudet University
Ms. Nancy Bloch, Director (202) 651-5312
Small Business Development Center
Management Institute
800 Florida Avenue, N.E.
Washington, D.C. 20002-3625

George Washington University
Ms. Susan Jones, Director (202) 994-7463
Small Business Development Center
National Law Center
720 20th Street, N.W.: Suite SL-101B
Washington, D.C. 20052

National Business League of
Southern Maryland, Inc.
Ms. Charlie Partridge, Director (301) 772-3683
Small Business Development Center
9200 Basil Court, Suite 210
Landover, Maryland 20785

FLORIDA

Florida Small Business Development Center
Mr. Jerry Cartwright, State Director (904) 474-3016
FAX: (904) 474-2030
UNIVERSITY OF WEST FLORIDA
11000 University Parkway
Pensacola, Florida 32514

Small Business Development Center
Mr. Walter Craft, Manager (904) 244-1036
414 Mary Esther Cutoff
Fort Walton Beach, Florida 32548

Florida A & M University
Ms. Patricia McGowan, Director (904) 599-3407
Small Business Development Center
1715-B South Gadsden Street
Tallahassee, Florida 32301

Florida Atlantic University
Mr. Mark Hosang, Director (407) 367-2273
Small Business Development Center
Building T-9, P.O. Box 3091
Boca Raton, Florida 33431

Energy Conservation Assistance Program
Mr. Ray Zentis, Director (407) 367-2273
Florida Atlantic University
Small Business Development Center
Building T-9: P.O. Box 3091
Boca Raton, Florida 33431

Florida Atlantic University
Mr. John Hudson, Director (305) 771-6520
Commercial Campus
Small Business Development Center
1515 West Commercial Blvd., Room 11
Fort Lauderdale, Florida 33309

Office of International Trade
Ms. Linda Krepel, Director (407) 367-2271
Florida Atlantic University
Small Business Development Center
Building T-9: P.O. Box 3091
Boca Raton, Florida 33431

Indian River Community College
Ms. Sharon Scott, Director (407) 468-4756
Small Business Development Center
3209 Virginia Avenue, 114
Ft. Pierce, Florida 34981-5599

Small Business Development Center
Ms. Bobbie McGee, Director (407) 837-5311
Prospect Place, Suite 123
3111 South Dixie Highway
West Palm Beach, Florida 33405

Florida International University
Mr. Marvin Nesbit, Director (305) 348-2272
Small Business Development Center
Trailer MO1 - Tamiami Campus
Miami, Florida 33199

Florida International University
Mr. Royland Jarrett, Manager (305) 940-5790
Small Business Development Center
NE 151 & Biscayne Boulevard
North Miami Campus
Academic Building #1, Room 350
Miami, Florida 33181

Small Business Development Center
Mr. William Healy, Manager (305) 987-0100
46 S.W. First Avenue
Dania, Florida 33304

Procurement Technical Assistance Program
Mr. Pete Singletary, Director (904) 474-2919
Small Business Development Center
11000 University Parkway: Building 8
Pensacola, Florida 32514

Product Innovation Center
Ms. Pamela Riddle, Director (904) 462-3942
The Progress Center
Small Business Development Center
#1 Progress Blvd., Box 7
Alachua, Florida 32615

University of Central Florida
Mr. Al Polfer, Director (407) 823-5554
Small Business Development Center
P.O. Box 25000: Building Ceba II
Orlando, Florida 32816

Brevard Community College
Ms. Vicki Peake, Director (407) 254-0305
Small Business Development Center
3865 North Wickham Road
Melbourne, Florida 32935

Seminole Community College
Mr. Glen Morgan, Director (407) 834-4404
Small Business Development Center
P.O. Box 150784
Altamonte Springs, Florida 32715-0784

Small Business Development Center
vacant (407) 951-1060
1519 Clearlake Road
Cocoa, Florida 32922

Stetson University
Mr. David Cross, Director (407) 822-7326
Small Business Development Center
School of Business Administration: P.O. Box 8417
DeLand, Florida 32720

University of North Florida
Dr. Lowell Salter, Director (904) 646-2476
Small Business Development Center
College of Business
4567 St. John's Bluff Road,
South: Building 11, Room 2163
Jacksonville, Florida 32216

Central Florida Community College
Mr. William Stensgaard, Manager (904) 377-5621
Small Business Development Center
214 West University Avenue: P.O. Box 2518
Gainesville, Florida 32601

University of South Florida
Mr. William Manck, Director (813) 974-4274
Small Business Development Center
College of Business Administration
4202 East Fowler Avenue, BSN 3403
Tampa, Florida 33620

Small Business Development Center
Mr. William Manck, Acting Manager (813) 359-4292
5700 North Tamiami Trail
Sarasota, Florida 33580

University of South Florida
vacant (813) 489-4140
Small Business Development Center
Sabel Hall, Rooms 219 & 220
8111 College Parkway
Fort Myers, Florida 33919

University of South Florida
vacant (813) 893-9529
Small Business Development Center
St. Petersburg Campus
830 First Street South, Room 113
St. Petersburg, Florida 33701

University of West Florida
Mr. Donald M. Clause, Director (904) 474-2908
Small Business Development Center
11000 University Parkway: Building 8
Pensacola, Florida 32514

GEORGIA

Georgia Small Business Development Center
Mr. Hank Logan, State Director
(404) 542-5760 FAX: (404) 542-6776
UNIVERSITY OF GEORGIA
Chicopee Complex: 1180 East Broad Street
Athens, Georgia 30602

North Georgia Regional
Mr. Harold Roberts, Director (404) 542-7436
Small Business Development Center
Chicopee Complex
1180 East Broad Street
Athens, Georgia 30602

Decatur Area Office
Ms. Carlotta Roberts, Coordinator (404) 378-8000
Small Business Development Center
750 Commerce Drive
Decatur, Georgia 30030

Gainesville Area Office
Mr. James C. Smith, Coordinator (404) 536-7984
Small Business Development Center
Brenau College, Butler Hall: Box 4517
Gainesville, Georgia 30501

Gwinnett Area Office
Ms. Susan Taylor, Coordinator (404) 963-4902
Small Business Development Center
1250 Atkinson Road
Lawrenceville, Georgia 30246

Central Georgia Regional
Mr. Charles Prickett, Director (912) 751-6592
Small Business Development Center
P. O. Box 13212
Macon, Georgia 31208

Southeast Georgia Regional
Mr. George Eckerd, Director (912) 264-7343
Small Business Development Center
1107 Fountain Lake Road
Brunswick, Georgia 31520

Savannah District Small Business
Mr. Harry O'Brien, Coordinator (912) 356-2755
Development Center
6555 Abercorn Extension, Suite 224
Savannah, Georgia 31405

Statesboro Area Office
Mr. David Lewis, Coordinator (912) 681-5194
Small Business Development Center
Georgia Southern College
Landrum Center, Box 8156
Statesboro, Georgia 30460

Southwest Georgia Regional
Ms. Linda Sue Ford, Director (912) 430-4303
Small Business Development Center
230 South Jackson Street: Suite 333
Albany, Georgia 31701

West Central Georgia District
Mr. Benno Rothschild, Director (404) 649-7433
Small Business Development Center
P.O. Box 2441
Columbus, Georgia 31902

Georgia State University
Mr. Lee Quarterman, Director (404) 651-3550
Small Business Development Center
Box 874: University Plaza
Atlanta, Georgia 30303

Augusta College
Mr. Marvin Doster, Director (404) 542-5760
Small Business Development Center
1180 East Broad Street
Augusta, Georgia 30602

Kennesaw State College
Mr. Gary Selden, Director (404) 423-6450
Small Business Development Center
P.O. Box 444
Marietta, Georgia 30061

Clayton State College
Mr. James W. Halloran, Director (404) 961-3440
Small Business Development Center
P.O. Box 285
Morrow, Georgia 30260

Floyd College District
Ms. Betty Nolen, Director (404) 295-6326
Small Business Development Center
P.O. Box 1864
Rome, Georgia 30163

HAWAII

Hawaii Small Business Development Center
Ms. Janet Nye, State Director
(808) 933-3515 FAX: (808) 933-3683
UNIVERSITY OF HAWAII AT HILO
523 West Lanikaula Street
Hilo, Hawaii 96720

Kaua'i Community College
Mr. Jim O'Donnell, Director (808) 245-8287
Small Business Development Center
3-1901 Kaumualii Highway
Lihue, Hawaii 96766

Maui Community College
Mr. David B. Fisher, Director (808) 242-7044
Small Business Development Center
310 Kaahumanu Avenue
Kahului, Hawaii 96732

University of Hawaii at Hilo
Mr. Frank A. Hatstat, Director (808) 933-3515
Big Island Center
Small Business Development Center
523 West Lanikaula Street
Hilo, Hawaii 96720

University of Hawaii at West O'ahu
at Business Action Center
Ms. Jean Williams, Director (808) 543-6695
Small Business Development Center
1130 North Nimitz Highway, Suite A254
Honolulu, Hawaii 96817

IDAHO

Idaho Small Business Development Center
Mr. Ronald R. Hall, State Director
(208) 385-1640 FAX: (208) 385-3877
BOISE STATE UNIVERSITY
College of Business 1-800-225-3815
1910 University Drive
Boise, Idaho 83725

Boise State University
Mr. Rod Grzadzieleski, Business Consultant
(208) 385-3875
Small Business Development Center
1910 University Drive
Boise, Idaho 83725

College of Southern Idaho
Ms. Cindy Brown, Director (208) 733-9554
Small Business Development Center
P.O. Box 1844
Twin Falls, Idaho 83303-1844

Idaho State University
Mr. Joe Pehrson, Director (208) 523-1087
Small Business Development Center
2300 North Yellowstone
Idaho Falls, Idaho 83401

Idaho State University
Mr. Paul Cox, Director (208) 232-4921
Small Business Development Center
1651 Alvin Ricken Drive
Pocatello, Idaho 83201

Lewis-Clark State College
vacant (208) 799-2465
Small Business Development Center
Eighth Avenue & Sixth Street
Lewiston, Idaho 83501

Panhandle Area Council
Mr. John Thielbahr, Business Consultant
(208) 263-4073
Small Business Development Center
Sandpoint Unlimited: P.O. Box 724
Sandpoint, Idaho 83864

Small Business Development Center
Mr. Jim Hunter, Director (208) 772-0587
Panhandle Area Council
11100 Airport Drive
Hayden, Idaho 83835

ILLINOIS

Illinois Small Business Development Center
Mr. Jeff Mitchell, State Director
(217) 524-5856 FAX: (217) 785-6328
DEPARTMENT OF COMMERCE &
COMMUNITY AFFAIRS
620 East Adams Street, 5th Floor
Springfield, Illinois 62701

Back of the Yards Neighborhood Council
Mr. Patrick Salmon, Director (312) 523-4419
Small Business Development Center
1751 West 47th Street
Chicago, Illinois 60609

Black Hawk Community College
Ms. Donna Scalf, Director (309) 762-3661
Small Business Development Center
c/o Illinois Quad Cities Chamber of Commerce
622 19th Street
Moline, Illinois 61265

Black Hawk College
Ms. Dorothy Henry, Director (309) 582-5373
Small Business Development Center
207 College Avenue
Aledo, Illinois 61231

Black Hawk Community College (East Campus)
Ms. Sharon Deahl, Director (800) 798-5671
Small Business Development Center
Business Resource Assistance Center: P.O. Box 489
Kewanee, Illinois 61443

Bradley University
Mr. Roger Luman, Director (309) 677-2309
Small Business Development Center
Lovelace Hall: 1501 West Bradley
Peoria, Illinois 61625

International Trade Center
Mr. Don Kudek, IT Specialist (309) 677-3075
Bradley University
Small Business Development Center
Lovelace Hall
Peoria, Illinois 61625

Chicago Area Neighborhood Development
Organizations (CANDO)
Ms. Pat Bell, Director (312) 939-7235
Small Business Development Center
343 South Dearborn Street, Suite 910
Chicago, Illinois 60604-3808

Chicago State University
Ms. Esther Crawford, Director (312) 995-3944
Small Business Development Center
95th and King Drive
Chicago, Illinois 60628

College of DuPage
Mr. Lee Pierce, Director (312) 858-2800
Small Business Development Center
22nd Street and Lambert Road
Glen Ellyn, Illinois 60137

International Trade Center
Ms. Jill Slager, IT Specialist (708) 858-2800
College of DuPage
Small Business Development Center
22nd Street and Lambert Road
Glen Ellyn, Illinois 60137

Cosmopolitan Chamber of Commerce
Ms. Connie Pope, Director (312) 786-0212
Small Business Development Center
1326 South Michigan Avenue
Chicago, Illinois 60605

Daley College
Ms. Judith Higgins-Gilbert, Director
(312) 838-0300
Small Business Development Center
7500 South Pulaski Road: Building 200
Chicago, Illinois 60652

Danville Area
Ms. Dianna Kirk, Director (217) 442-7232
Small Business Development Center
28 West North Street
Danville, Illinois 61832

Eighteenth Street Development Corporation
Mr. Chris Hall, Director (312) 733-2287
Small Business Development Center
1839 South Carpenter
Chicago, Illinois 60608

Elgin Community College
Mr. Craig Fowler, Director (708) 697-1000
Small Business Development Center
1700 Spartan Drive, Office B-15
Elgin, Illinois 60123

Evanston Business Investment Corporation
Mr. Tom Parkinson, Director (312) 866-1841
Small Business Development Center
1840 Oak Avenue
Evanston, Illinois 60201

Governors State University
Ms. Christine Cochrane, Director (312) 534-3713
Small Business Development Center
University Park, Illinois 60466

Greater North Pulaski Economic
Mr. Dan Immergluck, Director (312) 384-2262
Development Corporation
Small Business Development Center
4054 West North Avenue
Chicago, Illinois 60639

Greater Southwest Development Corporation
Ms. Pat Aleck, Director (312) 436-4448
Small Business Development Center
2358 West 63rd Street
Chicago, Illinois 60636

Hyde Park-Kenwood Development Corporation
Mr. Joel Werth, Director (312) 667-2610
Small Business Development Center
5307 South Harper
Chicago, Illinois 60615

Illinois Eastern Community Colleges
Ms. Debbie Chillson, Director (618) 395-3011
Small Business Development Center
1110 South West Street, Box 576
Olney, Illinois 62450

Illinois International Trade Center
Ms. Eve Baskowitz, Program Manager
(312) 814-2092
Dept. of Commerce & Community Affairs
Small Business Assistance Bureau
100 West Randolph, Suite 3-400
Chicago, Illinois 60601

Illinois State University
Ms. Nancy Verban, Director (309) 829-6632
Small Business Development Center
c/o McClean County Chamber of Commerce
210 South East Street
P.O. Box 1586 (mailing address)
Bloomington, Illinois 61702

Illinois Valley Community College
Mr. Boyd Palmer, Director (815) 223-1740
Small Business Development Center
Building 11, Route One
Oglesby, Illinois 61348

John Wood Community College
Mr. Edward Van Leer, Director (217) 228-5510
Small Business Development Center
301 Oak
Quincy, Illinois 62301

Joliet Junior College
Ms. Denise Mikulski, Director (815) 727-6544
Small Business Development Center
Renaissance Center, Room 319
214 North Ottawa Street
Joliet, Illinois 60431

Kankakee Community College
Mr. John O'Gorman, Director (815) 933-0374
Small Business Development Center
Box 888 River Road
Kankakee, Illinois 60901

Kaskaskia College
Mr. Richard McCullulm, Director (618) 532-2049
Small Business Development Center
Shattuc Road
Centralia, Illinois 62801

College of Lake County
Mr. Arthur Cobb, Jr., Director (708) 223-3633
Small Business Development Center
19351 West Washington
Grayslake, Illinois 60030

Lake Land College
Ms. Michele Paylor, Director (217) 235-3131
Small Business Development Center
South Route #45
Mattoon, Illinois 61938-9366

Latin/American Chamber of Commerce
Mr. Andrew Ramir, Director (312) 252-5211
Small Business Development Center
2539 North Kedzie, Suite 11
Chicago, Illinois 60647

Maple City Business and Technology Center
Ms. Carol Cook, Director (309) 734-4664
Small Business Development Center
620 South Main Street
Monmouth, Illinois 61462

Mid-Metro Economic Development Group
Ms. Anita Cibelli, Acting Director (708) 343-9205
Small Business Development Center
1505 West Lake Street
Melrose Park, Illinois 60160

Moraine Valley Community College
Ms. Hillary Gereg, Director (708) 974-5468
Small Business Development Center
Employment Training Center
10900 South 88th Avenue
Palos Hills, Illinois 60465

The Neighborhood Institute
Ms. Olivia M. Grady, Director (708) 933-2021
Small Buisness Development Center
2255 East 75th Street
Chicago, Illinois 60649

North River Commission
Mr. Joel Bookman, Director (312) 478-0202
Lawrence Avenue Dev. Corporation
Small Business Development Center
4745 North Kedzie
Chicago, Illinois 60625

Northern Illinois University
Mr. Larry Rouse, Director (815) 753-1403
Small Business Development Center
Department of Management: 305 East Locust
Dekalb, Illinois 60115

Olive-Harvey Community College
Mr. Jerry Chambers, Director (312) 660-4839
Small Business Development Center
10001 South Woodlawn Avenue
Chicago, Illinois 60628

Parkland College
Ms. Anita Bergman, Director (217) 351-2556
Small Business Development Center
2400 West Bradley Avenue
Champaign, Illinois 61821-1899

Rend Lake Community College
Mr. Robert Carlock, Director (618) 437-5321
Small Business Development Center
Upper Level, Student Center: Route #1
Ina, Illinois 62846

Richland Community College
Ms. Ticia Williams, Director (217) 875-7200
Small Business Development Center
One College Park
Decatur, Illinois 62521

Rock Valley College
Ms. Beverly Kingsley, Director (815) 968-4087
Small Business Development Center
1220 Rock Street, Suite 180
Rockford, Illinois 61101-1437

Sauk Valley Community College
Mr. Tom Gospodarczyk, Director (815) 288-5605
Small Business Development Center
173 Illinois Route #2
Dixon, Illinois 61021-9110

Shawnee College
Mr. Donald Denny, Director (618) 634-9618
Small Business Development Center
Shawnee College Road
Ullin, Illinois 62992

Southern Illinois University at Carbondale
Mr. Dennis Cody, Director (618) 536-2424
Small Business Development Center
Carbondale, Illinois 62901

Southern Illinois University at Edwardsville
Mr. Chuck Behn, Director (618) 692-2929
Small Business Development Center
Campus Box 1107
Center for Advanced Manufacturing and Production
Edwardsville, Illinois 62026

International Trade Center
Ms. Susan Inslee, IT Specialist (618) 692-2452
SIU at Edwardsville
Small Business Development Center
Campus Box 1107
Edwardsville, Illinois 62026

Southeast Chicago Development Commission
Ms. Lynne Cunningham, Director (312) 731-8755
Small Business Development Center
9204 South Commercial #212
Chicago, Illinois 60617

Spoon River College
Ms. Carrie McKillip, Director (309) 647-4645
Small Business Development Center: R.R. #1
Canton, Illinois 61520

University Village Association
Mr. Rand Arons, Director (312) 243-4045
Small Business Development Center
925 South Loomis Street
Chicago, Illinois 60607

Waubonsee Community College
Mr. Mike O'Kelley, Director (708) 892-3334
Small Business Development Center
Aurora Campus, 5 East Galena Blvd.
Aurora, Illinois 60506

Western Illinois University
Mr. Steven C. Roberts, Director (309) 298-1128
Small Business Development Center
216 Seal Hall
Macomb, Illinois 61455

Women's Business Development Center
Ms. Hedy Ratner and Carol Dougal, Directors
(312) 853-3477
Small Business Development Center
230 North Michigan Avenue, Suite 1800
Chicago, Illinois 60601

INDIANA

Indiana Small Business Development Center
Mr. Stephen Thrash, State Director
(317) 264-6871 FAX: (317) 264-3102
ECONOMIC DEVELOPMENT COUNCIL
One North Capitol, Suite 420
Indianapolis, Indiana 46204-2248

Columbus Enterprise Development Center, Inc.
Ms. Mary Schroeder, Director (812) 379-4041
Small Business Development Center
4920 North Warren Drive
Columbus, Indiana 47203

Evansville Chamber of Commerce
Mr. Jeff Lake, Director (812) 425-7232
Small Business Development Center
100 N.W. Second Street, Suite 206
Evansville, Indiana 47708

Fort Wayne Enterprise Center
Ms. Cheri Maslyk, Director (219) 426-0040
Small Business Development Center
1830 Wayne Trace
Fort Wayne, Indiana 46803

Greater Bloomington Chamber of Commerce
Mr. David Miller, Director (812) 339-8937
Small Business Development Center
116 West Sixth Street
Bloomington, Indiana 47404

Greater Lafayette Area
vacant (317) 742-0095
Small Business Development Center
224 Main Street
Lafayette, Indiana 47901

Hoosier Valley Economic Opportunity Corporation
Ms. Patricia Stroud, Director (812) 288-6451
Small Business Development Center
1613 East Eighth Street: P.O. Box 1567
Jeffersonville, Indiana 47130

Indiana State University
Mr. William Minnis, Director (812) 237-3232
Small Business Development Center
Terre Haute, Indiana 47809

Indiana University
Ms. Mary Alice McCord, Director (317) 274-8200
Small Business Development Center
1317 West Michriver
Indianapolis, Indiana 46202

Kokomo-Howard County Chamber of Commerce
Mr. Todd Moser, Director (317) 457-5301
Small Business Development Center
P.O. Box 731: 106 North Washington
Kokomo, Indiana 46903

LaPorte Small Business Development Center
vacant (219) 326-7232
321 Lincolnway
LaPorte, Indiana 46350

Madison Area Chamber of Commerce
Ms. Linda Heitz, Director (812) 265-3127
Small Business Development Center
301 East Street
Madison, Indiana 47250

Muncie-Delaware County Chamber
Ms. Nancy Stoll, Director (317) 284-8144
Small Business Development Center
P.O. Box 842: 401 South High Street
Muncie, Indiana 47308

NorthLake Small Business Development Center
vacant (219) 882-2000
504 Broadway, Suite 710
Gary, Indiana 46402
Northwest Indiana Forum, Inc.
Ms. Jeanennne Holcomb, Director (219) 942-3496
Small Business Development Center
8002 Utah Street
Merrillville, Indiana 46410

Project Future
Ms. Carolyn Anderson, Director (219) 282-4350
Small Business Development Center
300 North Michigan
South Bend, Indiana 46601

Richmond Area Chamber of Commerce
Ms. Patricia Stirn, Director (317) 962-2887
Small Business Development Center
600 Promenade Street
Richmond, Indiana 47374

IOWA

Iowa Small Business Development Center
Mr. Ronald Manning, State Director
(515) 292-6351 FAX: (515) 292-0020
IOWA STATE UNIVERSITY
College of Business Administration
137 Lynn Avenue
Ames, Iowa 50010

Drake University
Mr. Benjamin Swartz, Director (515) 271-2655
Small Business Development Center
Professional & Business Development Center
Lower Level
Des Moines, Iowa 50311

Dubuque Area Chamber of Commerce
Mr. Charles Tonn, Director (319) 588-3350
NE Iowa Small Business Development Center
770 Town Clock Plaza
Dubuque, Iowa 52001

Eastern Iowa Community College
Mr. Jon Ryan, Director (319) 322-4499
Small Business Development Center
304 West Second Street
Davenport, Iowa 52801

Indian Hills Community College
Mr. Bryan Ziegler, Director (515) 683-5127
Small Business Development Center
525 Grandview Avenue
Ottumwa, Iowa 52501

Southeastern Community College
Ms. Deb Dalziel, Branch Manager
(319) 752-2731
Small Business Development Center
Burlington Branch Office: Drawer F
West Burlington, Iowa 52655

Iowa Lakes Community College
Mr. Clark Marshall, Director (712) 262-4213
Small Business Development Center
Gateway North Shopping Center
Highway 71 North
Spencer, Iowa 51301

Iowa State University
Mr. Steve Carter, Director (515) 292-6355
Small Business Development Center
111 Lynn Avenue, Suite One
Ames, IA 50010

Audubon Branch Office
Mr. Marvin Dominick, Branch Manager
(712) 563-3165
Small Business Development Center
405 Washington Street
Audubon, Iowa 50025

Iowa Western Community College
Mr. Ronald Helms, Director (712) 325-3260
Small Business Development Center
2700 College Road, Box 4C
Council Bluffs, Iowa 51502

North Iowa Area Community College
Mr. Richard Petersen, Director (515) 421-4342
Small Business Development Center
500 College Drive
Mason City, Iowa 50401

Southwestern Community College
Mr. Paul Havick, Director (515) 782-4161
Small Business Development Center
1501 West Townline
Creston, Iowa 50801

University of Iowa/Oakdale Campus
Mr. Paul Heath, Director (800) 253-7232
Small Business Development Center
106 Technology Innovation Center
Iowa City, Iowa 52242

University of Northern Iowa
vacant (319) 273-2696
Small Business Development Center
Suite 5, Business Building
Cedar Falls, Iowa 50614-0120

Kirkwood Community College
Ms. Carol Thompson, Branch Manager
(319) 377-8256
Small Business Development Center
2901 Tenth Avenue
Marion, Iowa 52302

Western Iowa Tech Community College
Mr. Dennis Bogenrief, Director (712) 274-6400
Small Business Development Center
5001 East Gordon Drive, Box 265
Sioux City, Iowa 51102

KANSAS

Kansas Small Business Development Center
Mr. Tom Hull, State Director
(316) 689-3193 FAX: (316) 689-3647
WICHITA STATE UNIVERSITY
Campus Box 148
Wichita, Kansas 67208

Emporia State University
Ms. Lisa Brumbaugh, Regional Director
(316) 343-5308
Small Business Development Center
207 Cremer Hall
Emporia, Kansas 66801

Fort Hays State University
Ms. Clare Gustin, Regional Director
(913) 628-5340
Small Business Development Center
1301 Pine
Hays, Kansas 67601

Barton County Community College
Mr. Bruce Sloan, Director (316) 792-2701
Small Business Development Center
115 Administrative Building
Great Bend, Kansas 67530

Colby Community College
Mr. Robert Selby, Director (913) 462-3984
Small Business Development Center
1255 South Range
Colby, Kansas 67701

Garden City Community College
Mr. Vern Kinderknecht, Regional Director
(316) 276-9632
Small Business Development Center
801 Campus Drive
Garden City, Kansas 67846

Dodge City Community College
Mr. Harold Marconnette, Director (316) 225-1321
Small Business Development Center
2501 North 14th Avenue
Dodge City, Kansas 67801

Seward County Community College
Mr. Bob Carder, Director (316) 624-1951
Small Business Development Center
1801 North Kansas
Liberal, Kansas 67901

Johnson County Community College
Ms. Glenda Sapp, Regional Director (913) 469-3878
Small Business Development Center
CEC Building, Room 305I
Overland Park, Kansas 66210-1299

Kansas City Kansas Community College
Mr. Dan Pacheco, Director (913) 334-1100
Small Business Development Center
7250 State Avenue
Kansas City, Kansas 66112

Kansas State University
Mr. Fred Rice, Regional Director (913) 532-5529
Small Business Development Center
College of Business Administration
204 Calvin Hall
Manhattan, Kansas 66506

Kansas College of Technology
Mr. John Gosney, Regional Director (913) 825-0275
Small Business Development Center
2409 Scanlan Avenue
Salina, Kansas 67401

Pittsburg State University
Ms. Kathryn Richard, Regional Director
(316) 231-8267
Small Business Development Center
Shirk Hall
Pittsburg, Kansas 66762

University of Kansas
Mr. Mike O'Donnell, Regional Director
(913) 843-8844
Small Business Development Center
734 Vermont Street
Lawrence, Kansas 66044

Ottawa University
Ms. Lori Kravets, Director (913) 242-5200
Small Business Development Center
College Avenue, Box 70
Ottawa, Kansas 66067

Washburn University
Mr. Wayne Glass, Regional Director
(913) 295-6305
Small Business Development Center
School of Business
101 Henderson Learning Center
Topeka, Kansas 66621

Wichita State University
Mr. Chip Paul, Regional Director (316) 689-3193
Small Business Development Center
Brennan Hall, 2nd Floor: Campus Box 148
Wichita, Kansas 67208

Butler County Community College
Ms. Terri Courter, Director (316) 775-1124
Small Business Development Center
420 Walnut
Augusta, Kansas 67010

Cowley County Community College
Ms. Joan Warren, Director (316) 442-0430
Small Business Development Center
125 South Second
Arkansas City, Kansas 67005

Hutchinson Community College
Mr. Clark Jacobs, Director (316) 665-4950
Small Business Development Center
Ninth and Walnut, #225
Hutchinson, Kansas 67501

Pratt Community College
Mr. Pat Gordon, Director (316) 672-5641
Small Business Development Center
Highway 61
Pratt, Kansas 67124

KENTUCKY

Kentucky Small Business Development Center
Ms. Janet S. Holloway, State Director
(606) 257-7668 FAX: (606) 258-1907
UNIVERSITY OF KENTUCKY
Center for Business Development
205 Business and Economics Building
Lexington, Kentucky 40506-00341

Bellarmine College
Mr. Thomas Daley, District Director
(502) 452-8282
Small Business Development Center
School of Business
2001 Newburg Road
Louisville, Kentucky 40205-0671

Eastern Kentucky University
Mr. Donald R. Snyder, Director (606) 678-5520
South Central Small Business Development Center
107 W. Mt. Vernon Street
Somerset, Kentucky 42501

Elizabethtown Small Business Development Center
Mr. Denver Woodring, Director (502) 765-6737
238 West Dixie Avenue
Elizabethtown, Kentucky 42701

Morehead State University
Mr. Ernest Begley, Director (606) 783-2895
Small Business Development Center
207 Downing Hall
Morehead, Kentucky 40351

Ashland Small Business Development Center
Ms. Linda Akers, Director (606) 329-8011
Boyd-Greenup County Chamber of
Commerce Building
P.O. Box 830: 207 15th Street
Ashland, Kentucky 41105-0830

Pikeville Small Business Development Center
Mr. Michael Morley, Director (606) 432-5848
222 Hatcher Court
Pikeville, Kentucky 41501

Murray State University
Mr. Edward Davis, District Director
(502) 762-2856
West Kentucky Small Business
Development Center
College of Business & Public Affairs
Murray, Kentucky 42071

Hopkinsville Small Business
Development Center
Mr. Michael Cartner, Director (502) 886-8666
300 Hammond Drive
Hopkinsville, Kentucky 42240

Owensboro Small Business Development Center
Mr. Mickey Johnson, Director (502) 926-8085
3860 U.S. Highway 60 West
Owensboro, Kentucky 42301

Northern Kentucky University
Mr. Sutton Landry, Director (606) 572-6524
Small Business Development Center
BEP Center 463
Highland Heights, Kentucky 41099-0506

Southeast Community College
Mr. Cortez Davis, Director (606) 589-4514
Small Business Development Center
Room 113, Chrisman Hall
Cumberland, Kentucky 40823

University of Kentucky
Mr. William Morley, Director (606) 257-7666
Small Business Development Center
205 Business and Economics Building
Lexington, Kentucky 40506-00341

University of Louisville
Mr. Lou Dickie, Director (502) 588-7854
Small Business Development Center
Center for Entrepreneurship & Technology
School of Business: Belknap Campus
Louisville, Kentucky 40292

Western Kentucky University
Mr. Richard S. Horn, Director (502) 745-2901
Bowling Green Small Business Development Center
245 Grise Hall
Bowling Green, Kentucky 42101

LOUISIANA

Louisiana Small Business Development Center
Dr. John Baker, State Director
(318) 342-5506 FAX: (318) 342-5510
NORTHEAST LOUISIANA UNIVERSITY
College of Business Administration: Room 2-57
Monroe, Louisiana 71209-6435

Louisiana International Trade Center
Mr. Ruperto Chavarri, Coordinator
(504) 286-7197
University of New Orleans
368 Business Administration
New Orleans, Louisiana 70148

Louisiana State University at Shreveport
Ms. Charlotta Nordyke, Director (318) 797-5144
Small Business Development Center
College of Business Administration
One University Drive
Shreveport, Louisiana 71115

Louisiana Tech University
Mr. Art Gilbert, Director (318) 257-3537
Small Business Development Center
College of Business Administration
Box 10318, Tech Station
Ruston, Louisiana 71271-0046

Loyola University
Dr. Ronald Schroeder, Director (504) 865-3474
Small Business Development Center
College of Business Administration: Box 134
New Orleans, Louisiana 70118

McNeese State University
Mr. Paul Arnold, Director (318) 475-5529
Small Business Development Center
College of Business Administration
Lake Charles, Louisiana 70609

Nicholls State University
Dr. Aaron Caillouet, Director (504) 448-4242
Small Business Development Center
College of Business Administration
P.O. Box 2015
Thibodaux, Louisiana 70310

Northeast Louisiana University
Dr. Paul Dunn, Director (318) 342-1224
Small Business Development Center
College of Business Administration
Monroe, Louisiana 71209

Northeast Louisiana University
Dr. Jerry Wall, Special Project Director
(318) 342-1215
Louisiana Electronic Assistance Program
College of Business Administration
Monroe, Louisiana 71209

Northwestern State University
Ms. Mary Lynn Wilkerson, Director (318) 357-5611
Small Business Development Center
College of Business Administration
Natchitoches, Louisiana 71209

Alexandria Small Business Development Center
Ms. Kathey Hunter, Assistant Director
(318) 487-5454
5212 Rue Verdun
Alexandria, Louisiana 71306

Southeastern Louisiana University
Dr. John Crain, Director (504) 549-3831
Small Business Development Center
College of Business Administration
Box 522, SLU Station
Hammond, Louisiana 70402

Southern University
Ms. Vicki Bolden, Director (504) 922-0998
Capital Small Business Development Center
9613 Interline Avenue
Baton Rouge, Louisiana 70809

Southern University at New Orleans
Mr. Jon Johnson, Director (504) 286-5308
Small Business Development Center
College of Business Administration
New Orleans, Louisiana 70126

University of New Orleans
Dr. Ivan J. Miestchovich, Jr., Director
(504) 286-6978
Small Business Development Center
College of Business Administration
Lakefront Campus
New Orleans, Louisiana 70148

University of Southwestern Louisiana
Mr. Dan Lavergne, Director (318) 265-5344
Acadian Small Business Development Center
College of Business Administration: Box 43732
Lafayette, Louisiana 70504

MAINE

Maine Small Business Development Center
Ms. Diane Branscomb, Acting State Director
(207) 780-4420 FAX: (207) 780-4810
UNIVERSITY OF SOUTHERN MAINE
15 Surrenden Street
Portland, Maine 04101

Androscoggin Valley Council of
Governments (AVCOG)
Mr. John Jaworski, Director (207) 783-9186
Small Business Development Center
125 Manley Road
Auburn, Maine 04210

Coastal Enterprises Incorporated
Mr. James Burbank, Director (207) 882-7552
Small Business Development Center
Water Street: P.O. Box 268
Wiscasset, Maine 04578

Eastern Maine Development Corporation
Mr. Charles Davis, Director (207) 942-6389
Small Business Development Center
One Cumberland Place, Suite 300
Bangor, Maine 04402-2579

North Kennebec Regional Planning Commission
Mr. Elery Keene, Director (207) 873-0711
Small Business Development Center
Seven Benton Avenue
Winslow, Maine 04901

Northern Maine Regional Planning Commission
Mr. Robert P. Clark, Director (207) 498-8736
Small Business Development Center: P.O. Box 779
Caribou, Maine 04736

Southern Maine Regional Planning Commission
Ms. Madge Baker, Director (207) 324-0316
Small Business Development Center
255 Main Street: P.O. Box Q
Sanford, Maine 04073

University of Maine at Machias
Dr. William Little, Director (207) 255-3313
Small Business Development Center
Math and Science Building
Machias, Maine 04654

MARYLAND

Maryland Small Business Development Center
Mr. Michael E. Long, State Director (301) 333-6996
DEPT. OF ECONOMIC AND
EMPLOYMENT DEVELOPMENT
1-800-873-7273 FAX: (301) 333-6608
217 East Redwood Street, Tenth Floor
Baltimore, Maryland 21202

Central Region Small Business Development Center
Dr. John Faris, Director (301) 234-0505
1414 Key Highway: Suite 310, Box #9
Baltimore, Maryland 21230

Montgomery College
Ms. Janice Carmichael, Director (301) 656-7482
Small Business Development Center
7815 Woodmount Avenue
Bethesda, Maryland 20814

Salisbury State University
Dr. Richard Palmer, Director 1-800-999-SBDC
Small Business Development Center
1101 Camden Avenue
Salisbury, Maryland 21801

Southern Region Small Business Development Center
Ms. Yolanda Fleming, Director
(301) 932-4155 1-800-762-SBDC
235 Smallwood Village Shopping Center
Waldorf, Maryland 20602

Western Region Small Business Development Center
Mr. Robert Douglas, Director (301) 724-6716
Three Commerce Drive
Cumberland, Maryland 21502

MASSACHUSETTS

Massachusetts Small Business Development Center
Mr. John Ciccarelli, State Director
(413) 545-6301 FAX: (413) 545-1273
UNIVERSITY OF MASSACHUSETTS
School of Management, Room 205
Amherst, Massachusetts 01003

International Trade Program
Mr. John Ciccarelli, Director (413) 545-6301
University of Massachusetts
Small Business Development Center
School of Management, Room 205
Amherst, Massachusetts 01003

Boston College
Dr. Jack McKiernan, Regional Director
(617) 552-4091
Metropolitan Boston Regional Small
Business Development Center
96 College Road - Rahner House
Chestnut Hill, Massachusetts 02167

Boston College
Mr. Don Rielly, Director (617) 552-4091
Capital Formation Service Small
Business Development Center
96 College Road - Rahner House
Chestnut Hill, Massachusetts 02167

Clark University
vacant (508) 793-7615
Central Regional Small Business
Development Center
Graduate School of Management
950 Main Street
Worcester, Massachusetts 01610

Salem State College
vacant (508) 741-6639
North Shore Regional Small Business
Development Center
292 Loring Avenue, Alumni House
Salem, Massachusetts 01970

Southeastern Massachusetts University
Mr. Clyde L. Mitchell, Regional Director
(508) 673-9783
Small Business Development Center
200 Pocasset Street - P.O. Box 2785
Fall River, Massachusetts 02722

University of Massachusetts
vacant (413) 737-6712
Western Regional Small Business
Development Center
101 State Street, Suite 424
Springfield, Massachusetts 01103

Minority Business Assistance Center
Mr. Joseph France, Director (617) 287-7018
University of Massachusetts
Small Business Development Center
250 Stuart Street, 12th Floor
Boston, Massachusetts 02116

MICHIGAN

Michigan Small Business Development Center
Dr. Norman J. Schlafmann, State Director
(313) 577-4848 FAX: (313) 577-4222
WAYNE STATE UNIVERSITY
2727 Second Avenue
Detroit, Michigan 48201

Downriver Community Conference
Mr. Clifford Zanley, Director (313) 281-0700
Small Business Development Center
15100 Northline Road
Southgate, Michigan 48192

Ferris State University
Ms. Lora Swenson, Director (616) 592-3553
Small Business Development Center
Alumni 226: 901 South State Street
Big Rapids, Michigan 49307

First Step, Incorporated
Mr. David Gillis, Director (906) 786-9234
Small Business Development Center
2415 14th Avenue, South
Escanaba, Michigan 49829

Grand Rapids Community College
Mr. Douglas Smith, Director (616) 771-3600
Small Business Development Center
Applied Technology Center
Grand Rapids, Michigan 49503

Handicapper Small Business Association
Ms. Roseanne Herzog, Director (517) 484-8440
Small Business Development Center
1900 South Cedar, Suite 112
Lansing, Michigan 48910

International Trade Business Development Center
Mr. Myron Miller, Director
(517) 353-4336 1-800 852-5727
Michigan State University
Six Kellogg Center
East Lansing, Michigan 48824-1022

Kalamazoo College
Mr. Kenneth R. Warren, Director (616) 383-8602
Small Business Development Center
Stryker Center for Management Studies
1327 Academy Street
Kalamazoo, Michigan 49007

Kellogg Community College
Mr. Mark O'Connel, Director
(616) 965-3023 1-800 955-4KCC
Small Business Development Center
450 North Avenue
Battle Creek, Michigan 49107-3397

Lake Michigan Community College
Mr. James Converse, Acting Director (616) 927-3571
Small Business Development Center
Corporation and Community Development
2755 East Napier
Benton Harbor, Michigan 49022-1899

Lansing Communitiy College
Mr. Deleski Smith, Director (517) 483-1921
Small Business Development Center
P.O. Box 40010
Lansing, Michigan 48901

Livingston County Small Business Development
Center
Mr. Dennis Whitney, Director (517) 546-4020
404 East Grand River
Howell, Michigan 48843

Macomb County Small Business Development Center
Mr. Donald Morandini, Director (313) 469-5118
115 South Groesbeck Highway
Mt. Clemens, Michigan 48043

MERRA Small Business Development Center
Mr. Mark Clevey, Director (313) 930-0034
2200 Commonwealth, Suite 230
Ann Arbor, Michigan 48105

Michigan Technological University
Mr. James Hainault, Program Manager (906) 487-2470
Small Business Development Center
Bureau of Industrial Development
1400 Townsend Drive
Houghton, Michigan 49931

Forest Products Industry Assistance Center
Mr. Richard Tieder, Bureau Director (906) 487-2470
Michigan Technological University
Small Business Development Center
Bureau of Industrial Development
1700 College Aveune
Houghton, Michigan 49931

Muskegon Economic Growth Alliance
Mr. Vance Pattenger, Director (616) 722-3751
Small Business Development Center
349 West Webster Avenue, Suite 104: P.O. Box 1087
Muskegon, Michigan 49443-1087

Northern Michigan University
Mr. Allen Raymond, Director (906) 228-5571
Small Business Development Center
1009 West Ridge Street
Marquette, Michigan 49855

Northwestern Michigan College
Mr. Richard Wolin, Director (616) 922-1719
Small Business Development Center
1701 East Front Street
Traverse City, Michigan 49685

Ottawa County Economic
Development Office, Inc.
Mr. Ken Rizzio, Director (616) 892-4120
Small Business Development Center
6676 Lake Michigan Drive: P.O. Box 539
Allendale, Michigan 49401

Saginaw Area Growth Alliance
Mr. Steve Jonas, Coordinator (517) 754-8222
Small Business Development Center
301 East Genesee, Fourth Floor
Saginaw, Michigan 48607

Saint Clair County Community College
Mr. Robert F. Stevens, Director (313) 984-3881
Small Business Development Center
323 Erie Street
Port Huron, Michigan 48060

Thumb Area Community Growth Alliance
Mr. Marvin Pichla, Director (517) 635-3561
Small Business Development Center
3270 Wilson Street
Marlette, Michigan 48453

Walsh/O.C.C. Business Enterprise
Development Center
Ms. Dorothy Heyart, Director (313) 689-4094
3838 Livernois Road
Troy, Michigan 48007-7006

Wayne State University
Mr. Raymond Genick, Director (313) 577-4850
Small Business Development Center
School of Business Administration
2727 Second Avenue
Detroit, Michigan 48201

Comerica Small Business Development Center
Ms. Maria Hildreth, Director (313) 371-1680
8300 Van Dyke
Detroit, Michigan 48213

Manufacturers Reach Small Business
Development Center
Ms. Dorothy Benedict, Director (313) 869-2120
1829 Pilgrim
Detroit, Michigan 48223

NILAC-Marygrove College
Mr. Mark Carley, Director (313) 345-2159
Small Business Development Center
8425 West McNichols
Detroit, Michigan 48221

MINNESOTA

Minnesota Small Business Development Center
Mr. Randall Olsen, State Director
(612) 297-5770 FAX: (612) 296-1290
DEPARTMENT OF TRADE AND
ECONOMIC DEVELOPMENT
900 American Center Building:
150 East Kellogg Blvd.
St. Paul, Minnesota 55101

Bemidji State University
Mr. Arthur R. Gullette, Director (218) 755-2750
Small Business Development Center
1500 Birchmont Drive, Northeast
Bemidji, Minnesota 56601

Itasca Development Corporation
Mr. Joe Wood, Director (218) 327-2241
Grand Rapids Small Business Development Center
19 Northeast Third Street
Grand Rapids, Minnesota 55744

Rainy River Community College
Mr. Duane F. Ommen, Director (218) 285-2255
Small Business Development Center
Highway 11 & 71
International Falls, Minnesota 56649

Thief River Falls Technical College
Ms. Jan Hoff, Director (218) 681-5424
Small Business Development Center
Highway One East
Thief River Falls, Minnesota 56701

Brainerd Technical College
Mr. Gordon Winzenburg, Director (218) 828-5302
Small Business Development Center
300 Quince Street
Brainerd, Minnesota 56401

Pine Technical College
Mr. John Sparling, Director (612) 629-7340
Small Business Development Center
1100 Fourth Street
Pine City, Minnesota 55063

Mankato State University
Mr. Gary Hannem, Director (507) 389-1648
Small Business Development Center
P.O. Box 145
Mankato, Minnesota 56001

Faribault City Hall
Mr. James Wolfe, Director (507) 334-2222
Small Business Development Center
208 Northwest First Avenue
Faribault, Minnesota 55021

Minnesota Project Innovation
Mr. Jim Swiderski, Director (612) 338-3280
Small Business Development Center
Supercomputer Center, Suite M100
1200 Washington Avenue, South
Minneapolis, Minnesota 55415

Moorhead State University
Mr. Len Sliwoski, Director (218) 236-2289
Small Business Development Center
P.O. Box 303
Moorhead, Minnesota 56563

Wadena Technical College
Mr. Paul Kinn, Director (218) 631-1502
Small Business Development Center
222 Second Street, Southeast
Wadena, Minnesota 56482

St. Cloud State University
Mr. Tim Allen, Director (612) 255-4842
Small Business Development Center
Business Resource Center
1840 East Highway 23
St. Cloud, Minnesota 56304

Mid Minnesota Development Commission
Mr. Greg Bergman, Director (612) 235-8504
Small Business Development Center
333 Sixth Street West
Willmar, Minnesota 56201

Southwest State University
Mr. Jack Hawk, Director (507) 537-7386
Small Business Development Center
Science and Technology Resource Center #105
Marshall, Minnesota 56258

University of Minnesota at Duluth
Mr. Robert Heller, Director (218) 726-8761
Small Business Development Center
10 University Drive, 150 SBE
Duluth, Minnesota 55811

Hibbing Community College
Ms. Carol Moore, Director (218) 262-6700
Small Business Development Center
1515 East 25th Street
Hibbing, Minnesota 55746

Mesabi Community College
Mr. Robert Wagner, Director (218) 749-7729
Small Business Development Center
9th Avenue & West Chestnut Street
Virginia, Minnesota 55792

University of St. Thomas
Mr. William Connelly, Director (612) 223-8663
Small Business Development Center
23 Empire Drive
St. Paul, Minnesota 55103

Dakota County Technical College
Mr. Tom Trutna, Director (612) 423-8262
Small Business Development Center
1300 145th Street East
Rosemount, Minnesota 55068

Hennepin Technical College
Ms. Betty Walton, Director (612) 550-7153
Small Business Development Center
1820 North Zenuim Lane
Plymouth, Minnesota 55441

Normandale Community College
Ms. Heather Huseby, Director (612) 830-6395
Small Business Development Center
9700 France Avenue South
Bloomington, Minnesota 55431

Northeast Metro Technical College
Mr. Bob Rodine, Director (612) 779-5764
Small Business Development Center
3554 White Bear Avenue
White Bear Lake, Minnesota 55110

Winona State University
Ms. Tracy Thompson, Director (507) 457-5088
Small Business Development Center
Somsen Hall, Room 101
Winona, Minnesota 55987

Red Wing Technical Institute
Mr. Ken Henricksen, Director (612) 388-4079
Small Business Development Center
Highway 58 at Pioneer Road
Red Wing, Minnesota 55066

Rochester Community College
Mr. Tony Sinkiewicz, Director (507) 285-7536
Small Business Development Center
Highway 14 East: 851 30th Avenue, Southeast
Rochester, Minnesota 55904

MISSOURI

Missouri Small Business Development Center
Mr. Max E. Summers, State Director
(314) 882-0344 FAX: (314) 884-4297
UNIVERSITY OF MISSOURI
300 University Place
Columbia, Missouri 65211

Central Missouri State University
Mr. Wes Savage, Director (816) 543-4402
Small Business Development Center
Grinstead #80
Warrensburg, Missouri 64093-5037

Center for Technology
Mr. Bernie Sarbaugh, Coordinator (816) 429-4402
Small Business Development Center
Central Missouri State University
Grinstead #80
Warrensburg, Missouri 64093-5037

Center for Technology & Business Development
Mr. Harry Zimmerman, Director (816) 543-4402
Small Business Development Center
Central Missouri University
Grinstead #80
Warrensburg, Missouri 64093-5037

Mineral Area College
Mr. Charles Luther, Director (314) 431-4593
Small Business Development Center: P.O. Box 1000
Flat River, Missouri 63601

Missouri Product Finder
Ms. Sharon Gulick, Director (314) 751-4892
Small Business Development Center: P.O. Box 118
301 West High, Room 720
Jefferson City, Missouri 65102

Missouri Southern State College
Mr. Jim Krudwig, Director (417) 625-9313
Small Business Development Center
#107 Matthews Hall: 3950 Newman Road
Joplin, Missouri 64801-1595

Northeast Missouri State University
Mr. Glen Giboney, Director (816) 785-4307
Small Business Development Center
207 East Patterson
Kirksville, Missouri 63501

Northwest Missouri State University
Mr. James H. MacKinnon, Director (816) 562-1701
Small Business Development Center
127 South Buchanan
Maryville, Missouri 64468

Rockhurst College
Ms. Judith Burngen, Director (816) 926-4572
Small Business Development Center
1100 Rockhurst Road
Kansas City, Missouri 64110-2599

Saint Louis University
Ms. Virginia Campbell, Director (314) 534-7232
Small Business State University
3642 Lindell Boulevard
Saint Louis, Missouri 63108

Southeast Missouri State University
Mr. Frank "Buz" Sutherland, Director (314) 290-5965
Small Business Development Center
222 North Pacific
Cape Girardeau, Missouri 63701

Southwest Missouri State University
Ms. Jan Peterson, Director (417) 836-5685
Small Business Development Center
Center for Business Research: Box 88 (mail)
901 South National
Springfield, Missouri 65804-0089

Three Rivers Community College
Mr. John Bonifield, Director (314) 686-3499
Small Business Development Center
3019 Fair Street
Business Incubator Building
Poplar Bluff, Missouri 63901

University Extension
Dr. Tom Buchanan, Director (314) 634-2824
Business and Industrial Specialists
Small Business Development Center
2507 Industrial Drive
Jefferson City, Missouri 65101

University of Missouri at Columbia
Mr. Frank Siebert, Director (314) 882-7096
Small Business Development Center
1800 University Place
Columbia, Missouri 65211

University of Missouri at Rolla
Dr. Pete Schmidt, Director (314) 341-4561
Small Business Development Center
223 Engineering Management Building
Rolla, Missouri 65401-0249

Center for Technology Transfer
and Economic Development
Mr. Don Myers, Director (314) 341-4559
University of Missouri at Rolla
Small Business Development Center
Room 104, Building 1, Nagogami Terrace
Rolla, Missouri 654041-0249

MISSISSIPPI

Mississippi Small Business Development Center
Mr. Raleigh Byars, State Director
(601) 232-5001 FAX: (601) 232-5650
UNIVERSITY OF MISSISSIPPI
Suite 216: Old Chemistry Building
University, Mississippi 38677

Copiah-Lincoln Community College
Mr. Bob D. Russ, Director (601) 445-5254
Small Business Development Center
Natchez Campus
Natchez, Mississippi 39120

Delta State University
Mr. John Brandon, Director (601) 846-4236
Small Business Development Center
P.O. Box 3235 DSU
Cleveland, Mississippi 38733

Hinds Community College
Ms. Marquerite Wall, Director (601) 638-0600
Small Business Development Center
1624 Highway 27
Vicksburg, Mississippi 39180

Itawamba Community College
Mr. Bobby Wilson, Director (601) 680-8515
Small Business Development Center
653 Eason Boulevard
Tupelo, Mississippi 38801

Jackson State University
Mr. Marvel Turner, Director (601) 968-2795
Small Business Development Center
Suite A-1, Jackson Enterprise Center
931 Highway 80 West
Jackson, Mississippi 39204

International Trade Center
Dr. Richard Baltz, Director (601) 968-2795
Jackson State University
Small Business Development Center
Suite A-1, Jackson Enterprise Center
Jackson, Mississippi 39204

Meridian Community College
Mr. J.W. (Bill) Lang, Director (601) 482-7445
Small Business Development Center
5500 Highway 19 North
Meridian, Mississippi 39307

Mississippi Delta Community College
Ms. Martha Heffner, Director (601) 378-8183
Small Business Development Center
1656 East Union Street
Greenville, Mississippi 38702

Mississippi Department of Economic
and Community Development
Mr. Van Evans, Director (601) 359-3179
Small Business Development Center: P.O. Box 849
Jackson, Mississippi 39205

Mississippi State University
Mr. Estel Wilson, Director (601) 325-8684
Small Business Development Center
P.O. Drawer 5288
Mississippi State, Mississippi 39762

Northeast Mississippi Community College
Mr. Giles McDaniel, Director (601) 728-7751
Cunningham Boulevard: Stringer Hall, 2nd Floor
Booneville, Mississippi 38829

Pearl River Community College
Ms. Lucy Betcher, Director (601) 544-0030
Small Business Development Center
Route 9, Box 1325
Hattiesburg, Mississippi 39401

University of Mississippi
Mr. Jeffrey Van Terry, Director (601) 234-2120
Small Business Development Center
Old Chemistry Building, Suite 216
University, Mississippi 38677

University of Southern Mississippi
Ms. Rebecca Montgomery, Director (601) 865-4544
Small Business Development Center
USM-Gulf Park Campus
Long Beach, Mississippi 39560

MONTANA

Montana Small Business Development Center
Mr. Evan McKinney, State Director
(406) 444-4780 FAX: (406) 444-2808
DEPARTMENT OF COMMERCE
1424 Ninth Avenue
Helena, Montana 59620

Billings Incubator Small Business
Development Center
Mr. Al Jones, Director (406) 245-9989
P.O. Box 7213
Billings, Montana 59101

Dawson Community College
Mr. Gary Mariegard, Director (406) 365-2377
Small Business Development Center: Box 421
Glendive, Montana 59330

Gallatin Development Corporation College
Mr. Darrell Berger, Director (406) 587-3113
Small Business Development Center
321 East Main, Suite 413
Bozeman, Montana 59715

Flathead Valley Community College
Mr. Daniel Manning, Director (406) 756-3833
Small Business Development Center
777 Grandview Drive
Kalispell, Montana 59901

High Plains Development Authority
Mr. Karl J. Dehn, PTA Officer (406) 454-1934
Small Business Development Center
(Procurement Only)
#2 Railroad Square Building
Great Falls, Montana 59403

Missoula Incubator Small Business
Development Center
Mr. Tess Whalen, Director (406) 728-9234
127 North Higgins, Third Floor
Missoula, Montana 59802

REDI
Mr. Ralph Kloser, Director (406) 782-7333
Small Business Development Center
305 West Mercury, Suite 211
Butte, Montana 59701

NEBRASKA

Nebraska Small Business Development Center
Mr. Robert Bernier, State Director
(402) 554-2521 FAX: (402) 554-3363
UNIVERSITY OF NEBRASKA AT OMAHA
College of Business Administation, Suite 407D
Omaha, Nebraska 68182-0248

Chadron State College
Mr. Cliff Hanson, Director (308) 432-6282
Small Business Development Center
Administration Building
Chadron, Nebraska 69337

Kearney State College - West Campus
Ms. Kay Payne, Director (308) 234-8344
Small Business Development Center
Business Department Office Building
Kearney, Nebraska 68849

Mid-Plains Community College
Ms. Maurine Gotch Vinton, Director (308) 534-5115
Small Business Development Center
416 North Jeffers, Room 26
North Platte, Nebraska 69101

Peru State College
Ms. Dottie Holliday, Director
(402) 872-2274 1-800 742-4412
Small Business Development Center
T.J. Majors Hall, Room 248
Peru, Nebraska 68421

University of Nebraska at Lincoln
Mr. Larry Cox, Director
(402) 472-3358 1-800 742-8800
Small Business Development Center, Suite 302
Cornhusker Bank, 11th & Cornhusker Hgwy.
Lincoln, Nebraska 68521

University of Nebraska at Omaha
Ms. Jacklyn Staudt-Netzle, Director (402) 595-2381
Small Business Development Center
Peter Kiewit Center
1313 Farnam-on-the-Mall, Suite 132
Omaha, Nebraska 68182-0248

Wayne State College
Mr. Terry Henderson, Director (402) 375-2004
Small Business Development Center - Connell Hall
Wayne, Nebraska 68787

Western Nebraska Community College
Mr. Jeff Reifschneider, Director (308) 635-7513
Small Business Development Center
Nebraska Public Power Building
1721 Broadway, Room 408
Scottsbluff, Nebraska 69361

NEVADA

Nevada Small Business Development Center
Mr. Sam Males, State Director
(702) 784-1717 FAX: (702) 784-4305
UNIVERSITY OF NEVADA RENO
College of Business Administration: Room 411
Reno, Nevada 89557-0100

Carson City Chamber of Commerce
Mr. Larry Osborne, Executive Director
(702) 882-1565
Small Business Development Center
1900 South Carson Street, #100
Carson City, Nevada 89701

Northern Nevada Community College
Mr. Tom Lee, Management Consultant
(702) 738-8493
Small Business Development Center
901 Elm Street
Elko, Nevada 89801

Tri-County Development Authority
Ms. Sharlet Berentsen, Director (702) 623-5777
Small Business Development Center
50 West Fourth Street
Winnemucca, Nevada 89445

University of Nevada at Las Vegas
Ms. Sharolyn Craft, Director (702) 738-0852
Small Business Development Center
College of Business and Economics
4505 Maryland Parkway
Las Vegas, Nevada 89154

University of Nevada at Reno
Mr. Mike Mooney, Extension Economist (702)
784-1679
Cooperative Extension Service
Small Business Development Center
College of Agriculture
Reno, Nevada 89557-0016

NEW HAMPSHIRE

New Hampshire Small Business Development Center
Ms. Helen Goodman, State Director
(603) 862-2200 FAX: (603) 862-4468
UNIVERSITY OF NEW HAMPSHIRE
108 McConnell Hall
Durham, New Hampshire 03824

Keene State College
Mr. Dick Gorges, Regional Manager (603) 358-2602
Small Business Development Center: Blake House
Keene, New Hampshire 03431

Plymouth State College
Ms. Janice Kitchen, Regional Manager (603) 535-2523
Small Business Development Center: Hyde Hall
Plymouth, New Hampshire 03264

Small Business Development Center
Mr. Robert Ebberson, Regional Manager
(603) 625-5691
Merrimack Valley Subcenter
University Center: 400 Commercial Street, Room 311
Manchester, New Hampshire 03101

Small Business Development Center
Ms. Liz Matott, Regional Manager (603) 444-1053
North County Subcenter: P.O. Box 786
Littleton, New Hampshire 03561

University of New Hampshire
Ms. Katherine McCormick, Regional Manager
(603) 743-3995
Small Business Development Center
Seacoast Subcenter - Kingman Farm
Durham, New Hampshire 03824

NEW JERSEY

New Jersey Small Business Development Center
Ms. Brenda B. Hopper, State Director
(201) 648-5950 FAX: (201) 648-1110
RUTGERS UNIVERSITY
Graduate School of Management
University Heights: 180 University Avenue
Newark, New Jersey 07102

Brookdale Community College
Mr. Bill Nunnally and Larry Novick,
Regional Co-Directors (908) 842-1900
Small Business Development Center
Newman Springs Road
Lincroft, New Jersey 07738

Greater Atlantic City Chamber of Commerce
Mr. William R. McGinley, Regional Director
(609) 345-5600 800 252-4322
Small Business Development Center
1301 Atlantic Avenue
Atlantic City, New Jersey 08401

Kean College of New Jersey
Ms. Mira Kostak, Regional Director
(908) 527-2954
Small Business Development Center
East Campus, Room 242
Union, New Jersey 07083

Mercer County Community College
Mr. Herbert Spiegel, Regional Director
(609) 586-4800
Small Business Development Center
James Kerney Campus: 120 North Broad Street
Trenton, New Jersey 08690

Rutgers University at Camden
Ms. Patricia Peacock, Ed.D., Director
(609) 757-6221
Small Business Development Center
Business & Science Building, 2nd Floor
Camden, New Jersey 08102

Rutgers University at Newark
Mr. Gordon Haym, Director (201) 648-5950
Small Business Development Center
University Heights
180 University Avenue, Third Floor
Newark, New Jersey 07102

Warren County Community College
Ms. Dianne L. Latona, Director (201) 689-7613
Skylands Small Business Development Center
Route 57 West, RD #1 Box 55A
Washington, New Jersey 07882

NEW MEXICO

New Mexico Small Business Development Center
Mr. Randy Grissom, State Director
(505) 438-1362 FAX: (505) 438-1237
SANTA FE COMMUNITY COLLEGE
P.O. Box 4187
Santa Fe, New Mexico 87502-4187

Albuquerque Technical Vocational Institute
Ms. Roslyn Block, Director (505) 768-0651
Small Business Development Center
525 Buena Vista, SE
Albuquerque, New Mexico 87106

Clovis Community College
Mr. Roy Miller, Director (505) 769-4136
Small Business Development Center
417 Schepps Boulevard
Clovis, New Mexico 88101

Eastern New Mexico University at Roswell
Mr. Eugene D. Simmons, Director (505) 624-7133
Small Business Development Center
#57 University Avenue: P.O. Box 6000
Roswell, New Mexico 88201-6000

Luna Vocational Technical Institute
Ms. Corine Leger, Director (505) 454-2595
Small Business Development Center
Luna Campus: P.O. Drawer K
Las Vegas, New Mexico 88701

New Mexico Junior College
Mr. Don Leach, Director (505) 392-4510
Small Business Development Center
5317 Lovington Highway
Hobbs, New Mexico 88240

New Mexico State University at Alamogordo
Mr. Dwight Harp, Director (505) 434-5272
Small Business Development Center
1000 Madison
Alamogordo, New Mexico 88310

New Mexico State University at Carlsbad
Mr. Larry Coalson, Director (505) 887-6562
Small Business Development Center
301 South Canal: P.O. Box 1090
Carlsbad, New Mexico 88220

New Mexico State University at Dona Ana
Mr. Michael Elrod, Director (505) 527-7566
Small Business Development Center
Box 30001 Department 3DA
3400 South Espina Street
Las Cruces, New Mexico 88003-0001

New Mexico State University at Grants
Mr. Clemente Sanchez, Director (505) 287-8221
Small Business Development Center
709 East Roosevelt Avenue
Grants, New Mexico 87020

Northern New Mexico Community College
Mr. Darien Cabral, Director (505) 753-7141
Small Business Development Center
1002 North Onate Street
Espanola, New Mexico 87532

San Juan College
Mr. Brad Ryan, Director (505) 326-4321
Small Business Development Center
203 West Main, Suite 201
Farmington, New Mexico 87401

Santa Fe Community College
Ms. Emily Miller, Director (505) 438-1343
Small Business Development Center
South Richards Avenue:
P.O. Box 4187
Santa Fe, New Mexico 87502-4187

Tucumcari Area Vocational School
Mr. Richard Spooner, Director (505) 461-4413
Small Business Development Center
824 West Hines: P.O. Box 1143
Tucumcari, New Mexico 88401

University of New Mexico at Gallup
Ms. Barbara Stanley, Director (505) 722-2220
Small Business Development Center
103 W. Highway 66: P.O. Box 1395
Gallup, New Mexico 87305

University of New Mexico at Los Alamos
Mr. Jim Greenwood, Director (505) 662-0001
Small Business Development Center
901 18th Street, #18: P.O. Box 715
Los Alamos, New Mexico 87544

University of New Mexico at Valencia
Mr. Andrew Thompson, Director (505) 865-9596
Small Business Development Center
280 La Entrada
Los Lunas, New Mexico 87031

Western New Mexico University
Ms. Linda K. Jones, Director (505) 538-6320
Small Business Development Center
Phelps Dodge Building: P. O. Box 2672
Silver City, New Mexico 88062

NEW YORK

New York Small Business Development Centers
Mr. James L. King, State Director
(518) 443-5398 800-732-SBDC FAX: (518) 465-4992
STATE UNIVERSITY OF NEW YORK (SUNY)
SUNY Plaza, S-523
Albany, New York 12246

Corning Community College
Ms. Judy Smith, Director (607) 962-9461
Small Business Development Center
24-28 Denison Parkway West
Corning, New York 14830

Greater Syracuse Incubator Center
Mr. Robert Varney, Director (315) 475-0083
Small Business Development Center
1201 East Fayette Street
Syracuse, New York 13210

Jamestown Community College
Ms. Irene DoBies, Director
(716) 665-5220 800-522-7232
Small Business Development Center: P.O. Box 20
Jamestown, New York 14702-0020

Jefferson Community College
Mr. John F. Tanner, Director (315) 782-9262
Small Business Development Center
Watertown, New York 13601

Long Island University
Mr. Thomas Canavan, Director (718) 852-1197
Small Business Development Center
Humanities Building, Seventh Floor
One University Plaza
Brooklyn, New York 11201

Manhattan College
Mr. Frederick Greene, Director (212) 884-1880
Small Business Development Center: Farrell Hall
Riverdale, New York 10471

Monroe Community College
Ms. Colette Dorais, Director (716) 424-5200
Small Business Development Center
1000 East Henrietta Road
Rochester, New York 14623

Niagara Community College
Mr. Wilfred Bordeau, Director (716) 693-1910
Small Business Development Center
3111 Saunders Settlement Road
Sanborn, New York 14132

Pace University
Mr. William J. Lawrence, Director (212) 346-1899
Small Business Development Center: Pace Plaza
New York, New York 10038

Rockland Community College
Mr. Thomas J. Morley, Director (914) 356-0370
Small Business Development Center:
145 College Road
Suffern, New York 10901

State University at Stony Brook
Ms. Judith McEvoy, Director (516) 632-9070
Small Business Development Center
Harriman Hall, Room 109
Stony Brook, New York 11794

State University College at Buffalo
Ms. Susan McCartney, Director (716) 878-4030
Small Business Development Center: BA 117
1300 Elmwood Avenue
Buffalo, New York 14222

State University College at Plattsburg
Mr. Allan Wesler, Director (518) 564-7232
Small Business Development Center
Plattsburgh, New York 12901

State University College of Technology
at Farmingdale
Mr. Joseph Schwartz, Director (516) 420-2765
Small Business Development Center
Laffin Administration Building: Room 007
Farmingdale, New York 11735

State University Institute of Technology
at Utica/Rome
Mr. Thomas Reynolds, Director
(315) 792-7546
Small Business Development Center
P.O. Box 3050
Utica, New York 13504-3050

State University of New York at Albany
Mr. Peter George, Director (518) 442-5577
Small Business Development Center
Draper Hall, 107: 135 Western Avenue
Albany, New York 12222

State University of New York at Binghamton
Ms. Joanne Bauman, Acting Director
(607) 777-4024
Small Business Development Center
P.O. Box 6000
Vestal Parkway East
Binghamton, New York 13902-6000

Ulster County Community College
Mr. Michael Kirtio, Acting Director (914) 687-5272
Small Business Development Center
Stone Ridge, New York 12484

York College/City University of New York
Mr. James A. Heyliger, Director (718) 262-2880
Small Business Development Center
Science Building, Room 107
Jamaica, New York 11451

NORTH CAROLINA

North Carolina Small Business Development Center
Mr. Scott R. Daugherty, State Director
(919) 571-4154 FAX: (919) 787-9284
UNIVERSITY OF NORTH CAROLINA
4509 Creedmoor Road, Suite 201
Raleigh, North Carolina 27612

Appalachian State University
Mr. Bill Dowe, Acting Regional Director
(704) 262-2095
Northwestern Region SBDC
Walker College of Business
Boone, North Carolina 28608

Eastern Carolina University
Mr. Walter Fitts, Regional Director (919) 757-6157
Eastern Region SBDC: Willis Building
Corner of First and Reade Streets
Greenville, North Carolina 27834

Elizabeth City State University
Mr. Earl Brown, Regional Director (919) 335-3247
Northeastern Region SBDC: P.O. Box 874
Elizabeth City, North Carolina 27909

Fayetteville State Continuing Education Center
Dr. Sid Gautam, Regional Director (919) 486-1727
Cape Fear Region SBDC: P.O. Box 1334
Fayetteville, North Carolina 28302

North Carolina A&T State University
Ms. Cynthia Clemons, Associate Regional Director
(919) 334-7005
Northern Piedmont Center (Eastern Office)
CH Moore Agricultural Research Center
Greensboro, North Carolina 27411

University of North Carolina at Charlotte
Dr. Jon Benson, Regional Director (704) 548-1090
Southern Piedmont Region SBDC
c/o The Ben Craig Center
8701 Mallard Creek Road
Charlotte, North Carolina 28262

University of North Carolina
Mr. Marcus C. King, Regional Director
(919) 571-4154
Research Triangle Park SBDC
4509 Creedmoor Road, Suite 201
Raleigh, North Carolina 27612

University of North Carolina at Wilmington
Mr. Ted Jans, Jr., Regional Director
(919) 395-3744
Southeastern Region SBDC
Room 131, Cameron Hall
601 South College Road
Wilmington, North Carolina 28403

Western Carolina University
Mr. Thomas E. McClure, Regional Director
(704) 227-7494
Western Region SBDC
c/o Center for Improving Mountain Living
Cullowhee, North Carolina 28723

Winston-Salem State University
Mr. Bill Dowe, Regional Director (919) 750-2030
Northern Piedmont Region SBDC: P.O. Box 13025
Winston-Salem, North Carolina 27110

NORTH DAKOTA

North Dakota Small Business Development Center
Mr. Walter (Wally) Kearns, State Director
(701) 777-3700 FAX: (701) 223-3081
UNIVERSITY OF NORTH DAKOTA
Gamble Hall, University Station
Grand Forks, North Dakota 58202-7308

Bismarck Regional Small Business
Development Center
Mr. Jan Peterson, Regional Director
(701) 223-8583
400 East Broadway, Suite 421
Bismarck, North Dakota 58501

Dickinson State College
Mr. Bryan Vendsel, Regional Director (701) 227-2096
Small Business Development Center
314 Third Avenue West, Drawer L
Dickinson, North Dakota 58602

Grand Forks Regional Small Business
Development Center
Mr. Gordon Snyder, Regional Director (701) 772-8502
1407 24th Avenue, South, Suite 201
Grand Forks, North Dakota 58201

Jamestown Area Business and Industrial
Development
Mr. John Grinager, Regional Director (701) 252-9243
Small Business Development Center
121 First Avenue, West: P.O. Box 1530
Jamestown, North Dakota 58402

Minot Chamber of Commerce
Mr. George Youngerman, Regional Director
(701) 852-8861
Small Business Development Center
1020 20th Avenue Southwest: P.O. Box 940
Minot, North Dakota 58702

OHIO

Ohio Small Business Development Center
Ms. Holly I. Schick, Acting State Director
(614) 466-2711 FAX: (614) 466-0829
DEPARTMENT OF DEVELOPMENT
30 East Broad Street: P.O. Box 1001
Columbus, Ohio 43226

Akron - WEGO
Ms. Barbara Lange, Director (216) 535-9346
Small Business Development Center
58 West Center Street: P.O. Box 544
Akron, Ohio 44309

Ashtabula County Economic
Development Council, Inc.
Ms. Charlene Brueggeman, Director (216) 576-9126
Small Business Development Center
36 West Walnut Street
Jefferson, Ohio 44047

Athens Small Business Development Center
Ms. Karen Patton, Director (614) 592-1188
900 East State Street
Athens, Ohio 45701

Chillicothe-Ross Chamber of Commerce
Ms. Donna Smith, Administrator (614) 772-4530
Small Business Development Center
165 South Paint Street
Chillicothe, Ohio 45601

Cincinnati Small Business Development Center
Mr. Bill Fioretti, Director (513) 948-2082
IAMS Research Park - MC189
1111 Edison Avenue
Cincinnati, Ohio 45216-2265

Clermont County Chamber of Commerce
Mr. Dennis Begue, Director (513) 753-7141
Small Business Development Center
4440 Glen Este-Withamsville Road
Cincinnati, Ohio 45245

Columbus Area Chamber of Commerce
Mr. Burton Schildhouse, Director (614) 221-1321
Small Business Development Center
37 North High Street
Columbus, Ohio 43216

Coshocton Area Chamber of Commerce
Ms. Blanche Tyree, Director (614) 622-5411
Small Business Development Center
124 Chestnut Street
Coshocton, Ohio 43812

Dayton Area Chamber of Commerce
Mr. Doug Peters, Director (513) 226-8230
Small Business Development Center
Chamber Plaza - Fifth and Main Streets
Dayton, Ohio 45402-2400

Department of Development
of the CIC of Belmont County
Mr. Donald Myers, Director (614) 695-9678
Small Business Development Center
100 East Main Street
St. Clairsville, Ohio 43950

Greater Cleveland Growth Association
Mr. Russ Molinar, Director (216) 621-3300
Small Business Development Center
200 Tower City Center/50 Public Square
P.O. Box 94095
Cleveland, Ohio 44115

Greater Steubenville Chamber of Commerce
Mr. Jeff Castner, Director (614) 282-6226
Small Business Development Center
630 Market Street: P.O. Box 278
Steubenville, Ohio 43952

Lakeland Community College
Mr. Larry Kramer, Director (216) 951-1290
Lake County Economic Development Center
Small Business Development Center
Mentor, Ohio 44080

Lawrence County Chamber of Commerce
Ms. Lou Ann Walden, Director (614) 894-3838
Small Business Development Center
U.S. Route 52 and Solida Road
P.O. Box 488
Southpoint, Ohio 45680

Lima Technical College
Mr. Jerry Beidenharn, Director (419) 229-5320
(Perry Building)
Small Business Development Center
545 West Market Street, Suite 305
Lima, Ohio 45801

Logan-Hocking Chamber of Commerce
Mr. David L. Derr, Director (614) 385-7259
Small Business Development Center
11 1/2 West Main Street - Box 838
Logan, Ohio 43138

Lorain County Chamber of Commerce
Mr. Dennis Jones, Director (216) 246-2833
Small Business Development Center
6100 South Broadway
Lorain, Ohio 44053

Marietta College
Ms. Phyllis Baker, Director (614) 374-4649
Small Business Development Center
Marietta, Ohio 45750

Marion Area Chamber of Commerce
Ms. Lynn Lovell, Director (513) 382-2181
Small Business Development Center
206 South Prospect Street
Marion, Ohio 45750

Miami University
Dr. Michael Broida, Director (513) 529-4841
Department of Decision Sciences
Small Business Development Center
336 Upham Hall
Oxford, Ohio 45056

Mid-Ohio Small Business Development Center
Mr. Fred Moritz, Administrator (419) 525-1614
193 North Main Street
Mansfield, Ohio 44902

Northwest Technical College
Mr. Don Wright, Director (419) 267-5511
Small Business Development Center
St. Route One, Box 246-A
Archbold, Ohio 43502

Ohio University
Ms. Marianne Vermeer, Director (614) 593-1797
Innovation Center
Small Business Development Center
One President Street
Athens, Ohio 45701

Portsmouth Area Chamber of Commerce
Mr. Tom Reeder, Director (614) 353-1116
Small Business Development Center
P.O. Box 509
Portsmouth, Ohio 45662

Sandusky City Schools
Mr. Robert Proy, Director 800-548-6507
Small Business Development Center
407 Decatur Street
Sandusky, Ohio 44870

Southern State Community College
Mr. Phillip Knueven, Director 800-628-7722
Small Business Development Center
100 Hobart Drive
Hillsboro, Ohio 45133

Terra Technical College
Mr. Joe Wilson, Director (419) 332-1002
Small Business Development Center
1220 Cedar Street
Fremont, Ohio 43420

Toledo Small Business Development Center
Mr. Martin Modrowski, Director (419) 243-8191
218 North Huron Street
Toledo, Ohio 43604

Tuscarawas Chamber of Commerce
Mr. Tom Farbizo, Director (216) 343-4474
Small Business Development Center
1323 Fourth Street, N.W.: P.O. Box 232
New Philadelphia, Ohio 44663

Upper Valley Joint Vocational School
Mr. Jon Heffner, Director (513) 778-8419
Small Business Development Center
8811 Career Drive: North County Road, 25A
Piqua, Ohio 45356

WSOS Community Action Commission, Inc.
Mr. Tom Blaha, Director (419) 352-7469
Small Business Development Center
P.O. Box 48
118 East Oak Street
Bowling Green, Ohio 43402

Wright State University
Dr. Tom Knapke, Director (419) 586-2365
Small Business Development Center
Lake Campus: 7600 State Route 703
Celina, Ohio 45882

Youngstown State University
Ms. Patricia Veisz, Manager (216) 742-3495
Cushwa Center for Industrial Development
Small Business Development Center
Youngstown, Ohio 44555

Zanesville Area Chamber of Commerce
Mr. Edgar Friend, Director (614) 452-4868
Small Business Development Center
217 North Fifth Street
Zanesville, Ohio 43701

OKLAHOMA

Oklahoma Small Business Development Center
Dr. Grady Pennington, State Director (405) 924-0277
800-522-6154 FAX: (405) 924-8531
SOUTHEASTERN OKLAHOMA STATE UNIVERSITY
Station A, Box 2584
Durant, Oklahoma 74701

East Central University
Mr. Tom Beebe, Director (405) 436-3190
Small Business Development Center
1036 East Tenth
Ada, Oklahoma 74820

Albert Junior College
Mr. Dean Qualls, Bus. Dev. Specialist (918) 647-4019
Small Business Development Center
1507 South McKenna
Poteau, Oklahoma 74953

Langston University
Mr. Robert Allen, Director (405) 466-3256
Minority Assistance Center
Small Business Development Center: P.O. Box 667
Langston, Oklahoma 73050

Northeastern Oklahoma State University
Dr. Constance Pogue, Director (918) 458-0802
Small Business Development Center
Tahlequah, Oklahoma 74464

Tulsa State Office Building
Mr. Jeff Horvath, Director (918) 581-2502
Small Business Development Center
440 South Houston, Suite 206
Tulsa, Oklahoma 74107

Northwestern Oklahoma State University
Mr. David Pecha, Director (405) 327-5883
Small Business Development Center
Alva, Oklahoma 73717

Phillips University
Mr. Bill Gregory, Bus. Dev. Specialist (405) 242-7989
Small Business Development Center
100 South University Avenue
Enid, Oklahoma 73701

Rose State College
Ms. Judy Robbins, Director (405) 733-7348
Small Business Development Center
6420 Southeast 15th Street
Midwest City, Oklahoma 73110

Southeastern Oklahoma State University
Mr. Herb Manning, Director (405) 924-0277
Small Business Development Center: 517 University
Durant, Oklahoma 74701

Southwestern Oklahoma State University
Mr. Chuck Felz, Director (405) 774-1040
Small Business Development Center
100 Campus Drive
Weatherford, Oklahoma 73096

American National Bank Building
Ms. Linda Strelecki, Bus. Dev. Specialist (405) 248-4946
Small Business Development Center
601 SW "D", Suite 209
Lawton, Oklahoma 73501

University of Central Oklahoma
Ms. Susan Urbach, Director (405) 359-1968
Small Business Development Center
100 North Boulevard
Edmond, Oklahoma 73034

OREGON

Oregon Small Business Development Center
Mr. Sandy Cutler, State Director
(503) 726-2250 FAX: (503) 345-6006
LANE COMMUNITY COLLEGE
99 West Tenth, Suite 216
Eugene, Oregon 97401

Blue Mountain Community College
Mr. Garth Davis, Director (503) 276-6233
Small Business Development Center
37 S.E. Dorian
Pendleton, Oregon 97801

Central Oregon Community College
Mr. Bob Newhart, Director (503) 385-5524
Small Business Development Center
2600 N.W. College Way
Bend, Oregon 97701

Chemeketa Community College
Ms. Bobbie Clyde, Director (503) 399-5181
Small Business Development Center
365 Ferry Street S.E.
Salem, Oregon 97301

Clackamas Community College
Mr. Bob Ellis, Director (503) 656-4447
Small Business Development Center
7616 S.E. Harmony Road
Milwaukee, Oregon 97222

Clatstop Community College
Ms. Robin Priddy, Director (503) 738-3347
Small Business Devleopment Center
1240 South Holladay
Seaside, Oregon 97138

Columbia George Community College
Mr. Bob Cole, Director (503) 296-1173
Small Business Development Center
212 Washington
The Dalles, Oregon 97058

Eastern Oregon State College
Mr. Terry Edvalson, Director 1-800-452-8639
Small Business Development Center
Regional Services Institute
LaGrande, Oregon 97850

Lane Community College
Ms. Jane Scheidecker, Director (503) 726-2255
Small Business Development Center
1059 Williamette Street
Eugene, Oregon 97401

Linn-Benton Community College
Mr. John Pascone, Director (503) 967-6112
Small Business Development Center
6500 S.W. Pacific Boulevard
Albany, Oregon 97321

Mount Hood Community College
Mr. Don King, Director (503) 667-7658
Small Business Development Center
323 N.E. Roberts Street
Gresham, Oregon 97030

Oregon Coast Community College
Mr. Patrick O'Connor, Director
(503) 994-4166 Service District
Small Business Development Center
4157 N.W. Highway 101: P.O. Box 419
Lincoln City, Oregon 97367

Oregon Institute of Technology
Ms. Jamie Albert, Director (503) 885-1760
Small Business Development Center
3201 Campus Drive, South 314
Klamath Falls, Oregon 97601

Portland Community College
Mr. Hal Bergmann, Director (503) 273-2828
Small Business Development Center
123 N.W. Second Avenue, Suite 321
Portland, Oregon 97209

Portland Community College
Mr. John Otis, Director (503) 274-7482
Small Business Int'l Trade Program
121 S.W. Salmon Street, Suite 210
Portland, Oregon 97204

Rouge Community College
Mr. Roger Harding, Director (503) 474-0762
Small Business Development Center
290 N.E. "C" Street
Grants Pass, Oregon 97526

Southern Oregon State College/Ashland
Ms. Liz Shelby, Director (503) 482-5838
Small Business Development Center
Regional Services Institute
Ashland, Oregon 97520

Southern Oregon State College/Medford
Mr. Jon Trivers, Director (503) 772-3478
Small Business Development Center
Regional Services Institute
229 North Bartlett
Medford, Oregon 97501

Southwestern Oregon Community College
Mr. C.J. (Siobhan) Gradenwitz, Director (503) 267-2300
Small Business Development Center
340 Central
Coos Bay, Oregon 97420

Tillamook Bay Community College
Mr. Bill Geiger, Director (503) 842-2551
Small Business Development Center
401 B Main Street
Tillamook, Oregon 97141

Treasure Valley Community College
Ms. Kathy Simko, Director (503) 889-2617
Small Business Development Center
88 S.W. Third Avenue
Ontario, Oregon 97914

Umpqua Community College
Mr. Terry Swagerty, Director (503) 672-2535
Small Business Development Center
744 S.E. Rose
Roseburg, Oregon 97470

PENNSYLVANIA

Pennsylvania Small Business
Development Center
Mr. Gregory L. Higgins, State Director
(215) 898-1219 FAX: (215) 898-1299
UNIVERSITY OF PENNSYLVANIA
The Wharton School
444 Vance Hall: 3733 Spruce Street
Philadelphia, Pennsylvania 19104

Bucknell University
Dr. Charles Coder, Director (717) 524-1249
Small Business Development Center
126 Dana Engineering Building
Lewisburg, Pennsylvania 17837

Clarion University of Pennsylvania
Dr. Woodrow Yeaney, Director (814) 226-2060
Small Business Development Center
Dana Still Building
Clarion, Pennsylvania 16214

Duquesne University
Dr. Mary T. McKinney, Director (412) 434-6233
Small Business Development Center
Rockwell Hall - Room 10 Concourse
600 Forbes Avenue
Pittsburgh, Pennsylvania 15282

Gannon University
Mr. Ernie Post, Director (814) 871-7714
Small Business Development Center
Carlisle Building, 3rd Floor
Erie, Pennsylvania 16541

LaSalle University
Ms. Linda Karl, Director (215) 951-1416
Small Business Development Center
19th West Olney Avenue: Box 365
Philadelphia, Pennsylvania 19141

Lehigh University
Mr. Larry Strain, Director (215) 758-3980
Small Business Development Center
301 Broadway - Route 230
Bethlehem, Pennsylvania 18015

Kutztown University SBDC
Dr. Keith Yackee, Director (717) 233-3120
Small Business Development Center
2986 North Second Street
Harrisburg, Pennsylvania 17110

St. Francis College
Mr. John A. Palko, Director
(814) 472-3200
Small Business Development Center
Business Resource Center
Loretto, Pennsylvania 15940

St. Vincent College
Mr. Jack Fabean, Director (412) 537-4572
Small Business Development Center
Alfred Hall, Fourth Floor
Latrobe, Pennsylvania 15650-2690

Temple University
Ms. Geraldine Perkins, Director (215) 787-7282
Small Business Development Center
Room Six, Speakman Hall - 006-00
Philadelphia, Pennsylvania 19122

University of Pennsylvania
Mr. David B. Thornburgh, Director (215) 898-4861
Small Business Development Center
The Wharton School: 409 Vance Hall
Philadelphia, Pennsylvania 19104-6357

University of Pittsburgh
Mr. Clarence K. Curry, Director (412) 648-1544
Small Business Development Center
Room 343 Mervis Hall
Pittsburgh, Pennsylvania 15260

University of Scranton
Ms. Elaine M. Tweedy, Director (717) 941-7588
Small Business Development Center
St. Thomas Hall, Room 588
Scranton, Pennsylvania 18510

Wilkes College
Mr. Edmund Sieminski, Director (717) 824-4651
Small Business Development Center
Hollenback Hall: 192 South Franklin Street
Wilkes-Barre, Pennsylvania 18766

RHODE ISLAND

Rhode Island Small Business Development Center
Mr. Douglas Jobling, State Director
(401) 232-6111 FAX: (401) 232-6319
Mr. Raymond Fogarty, Director,
Export Assistance Center (401) 232-6407
BRYANT COLLEGE: 1150 Douglas Pike
Smithfield, Rhode Island 02917-1284

Community College of Rhode Island
Ms. Judith Shea, Manager (401) 455-6042
Small Business Development Center
One Hilton Street
Providence, Rhode Island 02905

Downtown Providence Small Business
Development Center
Ms. Sue Barker, Assistant Director (401) 831-1330
270 Weybosset Street
Providence, Rhode Island 02903

University of Rhode Island
Mr. Thomas F. Policastro, Manager (401) 792-2451
Small Business Development Center
24 Woodward Hall
Kingston, Rhode Island 02881

SOUTH CAROLINA

South Carolina Small Business Development Center
Mr. John Lenti, State Director
(803) 777-4907 FAX: (803) 777-4403
Mr. James Brazell, Regional Director (803) 777-5118
UNIVERSITY OF SOUTH CAROLINA
College of Business Administration
1710 College Street
Columbia, South Carolina 29208

Aiken/North Augusta Small Business
Ms. Jackie Moore, Acting Area Manager
(803) 442-3670
Development Center: Triangle Plaza, Highway 25
North Augusta, South Carolina 29841

Trident Technical College
Mr. Tom Koontz, Area Manager (803) 727-2020
Small Business Development Center
66 Columbus Street: P.O. Box 20339
Charleston, South Carolina 29413-0339

University of South Carolina - Beaufort
Ms. Terry Murray, Area Manager (803) 524-7112
Small Business Development Center
800 Carteret Street
Beaufort, South Carolina 29902

Clemson University
Mr. Joey Nimmer, Regional Director (803) 656-3227
Small Business Development Center
Ms. Rebecca C. Hobart, Area Manager
College of Commerce and Industry: 425 Sirrine Hall
Clemson, South Carolina 29634-1301

Greenville Technical College
Ms. Harriette Edwards, Area Manager (803) 271-4259
Small Business Development Center
Box 5616, Station B, GHEC
Greenville, South Carolina 29606

Spartanburg Chamber of Commerce
Mr. Robert Grooms, Area Manager (803) 594-5080
Small Business Development Center: P.O. Box 1636
Spartanburg, South Carolina 29304

Upper Savannah Council of Government
Mr. George Long, Area Manager (803) 227-6110
Small Business Development Center
Exchange Building: 222 Phoenix Street, Suite 200
Greenwood, South Carolina 29648

South Carolina State College
Mr. John Gadson, Regional Director (803) 536-8445
Small Business Development Center
School of Business Administration: P.O. Box 1676
Orangeburg, South Carolina 29117

Winthrop College
Mr. Nate Barber, Regional Director (803) 323-2283
Small Business Development Center
School of Business Administration
119 Thurmond Building
Rock Hill, South Carolina 29733

Coastal Carolina College
Mr. Patrick King, Area Manager (803) 349-2169
Small Business Development Center
School of Business Administration
Conway, South Carolina 29526

Florence Darlington Technical College
Mr. David Raines, Area Manager (803) 661-8324
Small Business Development Center
P.O. Box 100548
Florence, South Carolina 29501

SOUTH DAKOTA

South Dakota Small Business Development Center
Mr. Donald Greenfield, State Director
(605) 677-5272 FAX: (605) 677-5427
UNIVERSITY OF SOUTH DAKOTA
School of Business
414 East Clark, Patterson 115
Vermillion, South Dakota 57069

Aberdeen Small Business Development Center
Mr. Ron Kolbeck, Area Director (605) 622-2252
226 Citizens Building
Aberdeen, South Dakota 57401

Pierre Small Business Development Center
Mr. Wade Druin, Area Director (605) 773-5941
105 South Euclid, Suite C
Pierre, South Dakota 57501

Rapid City Small Business Development Center
Mr. Bob Domalewski, Area Director (605) 394-5311
2525 West Main, Suite 105: P.O. Box 7715
Rapid City, South Dakota 57709

Sioux Falls Small Business Development Center
Mr. Jim Lemonds, Area Director (605) 339-3366
231 South Phillips, Room 365
Sioux Falls, South Dakota 57101

TENNESSEE

Tennessee Small Business Development Center
Dr. Kenneth J. Burns, State Director
(901) 678-2500 FAX: (901) 678-4072
MEMPHIS STATE UNIVERSITY
Memphis, Tennessee 38152

International Trade Center
Mr. Philip Johnson, Director (901) 678-4174
Memphis State University
Small Business Development Center
Memphis, Tennessee 38152

Austin Peay State University
Mr. John Volker, Director (615) 648-7764
Small Business Development Center
College of Business
Clarksville, Tennessee 37044-0001

Cleveland State Community College
Mr. Don Geren, Director (615) 478-6247
Small Business Development Center
Business and Technology: P.O. Box 3570
Cleveland, Tennessee 37320-3570

Dyersburg State Community College
Mr. Bob Wylie, Director (901) 286-3201
Small Business Development Center
Office of Extension Services: P.O. Box 648
Dyersburg, Tennessee 38024

East Tennessee State University
Mr. Bob Justice, Director (615) 929-5630
Small Business Development Center
College of Business: P.O. Box 23, 440A
Johnson City, Tennessee 37614-0002

Jackson State Community College
Ms. Deborah Bishop, Director (901) 424-5389
Small Business Development Center
2046 North Parkway Street
Jackson, Tennessee 38301-3797

Memphis State University
Mr. Earnest Lacey, Director (901) 527-1041
Small Business Development Center
320 South Dudley Street
Memphis, Tennessee 38104-3206

Middle Tennessee State University
Dr. Jack Forest, Director (615) 898-2745
Small Business Development Center
School of Business:
P.O. Box 487
Murfreesboro, Tennessee 37132

Pellissippi State Technical Community College
Mr. Joe Andrews, Director (615) 694-6660
Small Business Development Center
P.O. Box 22990
Knoxville, Tennessee 37933-0990

Tennessee State University
Mr. Billy E. Lowe, Director (615) 251-1178
Small Business Development Center
School of Business
Tenth and Charlotte Avenue
Nashville, Tennessee 37203

Tennessee Technological University
Mr. Harold Holloway, Director (615) 372-3648
Small Business Development Center
College of Business Administration
P.O. Box 5023
Cookeville, Tennessee 38505-0001

University of Tennessee at Martin
Mr. Carl Savage, Director (901) 587-7236
Small Business Development Center
402 Elm Street
Martin, Tennessee 38237-3415

Walters State Community College
Mr. Jack Tucker, Director (615) 587-9722
Small Business Development Center
Business/Industrial Services
500 South Davy Crockett Parkway
Morristown, Tennessee 37813-6889

TEXAS

Northeastern Texas Small Business
Development Center
Ms. Marty Jones, Region Director
(214) 565-5831 FAX: (214) 565-5857
DALLAS COUNTY COMMUNITY COLLEGE
1402 Corinth Street
Dallas, Texas 75215

Center for Government Contracting
Ms. Vera Tanner, Director (214) 565-5842
Small Business Development Center
1402 Corinth
Dallas, Texas 75215

Collin County Community College
Mr. Steve Hardy, Director (214) 881-0506
Small Business Development Center
Plano Market Square
1717 East Spring Creek Parkway, #109
Plano, Texas 75074

Cooke County College
Ms. Cathy Keeler, Director (817) 665-4785
Small Business Development Center
1525 West California
Gainesville, Texas 76240

Dallas County Community College
Mr. Al Salgado, Director (214) 565-5857
Small Business Development Center
1402 Corinth
Dallas, Texas 75215

Grayson County College
Mr. Jerry Linn, Director (903) 463-8654
Small Business Development Center
6101 Grayson Drive
Denison, Texas 75020

International Trade Center
Ms. Elizabeth Huddleston, Director (214) 653-1777
Small Business Development Center
World Trade Center, Suite #150
2050 Stemmons Freeway: P.O. Box 58299
Dallas, Texas 75258

Kilgore College
Mr. Chris A. Mullins, Director
(903) 753-2642 or 757-5857
Small Business Development Center
300 South High
Longview, Texas 75601

McLennan Community College
Ms. Lu Billings, Director (817) 750-3600
Small Business Development Center
4601 North 19th Street, Suite A-15
Waco, Texas 76708

Navarro Small Business Development Center
Mr. Gary M. Burns, Director (903) 874-0658
120 North 12th Street
Corsicana, Texas 75110

Northeast/Texarkana Small Business
Development Center
Mr. Bob Wall, Director (903) 572-1911
P.O. Box 1307
Mt. Pleasant, Texas 75455

Paris Junior College
Ms. Pat Bell, Director (903) 784-1802
Small Business Development Center
2400 Clarksville Street
Paris, Texas 75460

Tarrant County Junior College
Mr. James Emery, Director
(817) 877-9254 or 877-9278
Small Business Development Center
1500 Houston Street, Room 163
Ft. Worth, Texas 76102

Trinity Valley Community College
Ms. Judy Loden, Director (903) 675-6230
Small Business Development Center
500 South Prairieville
Athens, Texas 75751

Tyler Junior College
Mr. Glenn Galiga, Director (903) 510-2975
Small Business Development Center
1530 South S.W. Loop 323, Suite 100
Tyler, Texas 75701

UNIVERSITY OF HOUSTON
Dr. Elizabeth Gatewood, Region Director
(713) 752-8444
Small Business Development Center
Mr. Ted Cadou, Assistant Region Director
FAX: (713) 752-8484
601 Jefferson, Suite 2330
Houston, Texas 77002

International Trade Center
Mr. Luis Saldarriaga, Director (713) 752-8404
University of Houston
601 Jefferson, Suite 2330
Houston, Texas 77002

Alvin Community College
Ms. Gina Mattei, Director (713) 388-4686
Small Business Development Center
3110 Mustang Road
Alvin, Texas 77511-4898

Angelina Chamber of Commerce
Mr. Chuck Stemple, Director (409) 634-1887
Small Business Development Center
1615 South Chestnut: P.O. Box 1606
Lufkin, Texas 75901

Blinn College
Ms. Phillis Nelson, Director (409) 830-4137
Small Business Development Center
902 College Avenue
Brenham, Texas 77833

Brazosport College
Ms. Rhonda Wade, Director (409) 265-6131
Small Business Development Center
500 College Drive
Lake Jackson, Texas 77566

Bryan/College Station Chamber of Commerce
Mr. Frank Murphy, Director (409) 823-3034
Small Business Development Center
401 South Washington
Bryan, Texas 77803

College of the Mainland
Mr. Ed Socha, Director (409) 938-7578
Small Business Development Center
8419 Emmett F. Lowry Expressway
Texas City, Texas 77591

Galveston College
Mr. Mal Hunter, Director (409) 740-7380
Small Business Development Center
5001 Avenue U
Galveston, Texas 77550

Houston Community College System
Mr. John Fishero, Director (713) 499-4870
Small Business Development Center
13600 Murphy Road
Stafford, Texas 77477

Lamar University
Mr. Roy Huckaby, Director
(409) 880-2367 800-722-3443
Small Business Development Center
855 Florida Avenue
Beaumont, Texas 77705

Lee College
Mr. Kenneth Voytek, Director (713) 425-6309
Small Business Development Center: Rundell Hall
Baytown, Texas 77520-4796

North Harris Montgomery Community College
District
Mr. Ray Laughter, Director
(713) 359-1677 800-443-SBDC
Small Business Development Center
Administration Building, Room 104
20000 Kingwood Drive
Kingwood, Texas 77339

Texas Information Procurement Service
Mr. Ed Wilder, Director (713) 752-8477 800-252-7232
University of Houston
Small Business Development Center
401 Louisiana, 7th Floor
Houston, Texas 77002

Texas Product Development Center
Mr. Bob Maxfield, Director (713) 752-8400
University of Houston
Small Business Development Center
401 Louisiana, 7th Floor
Houston, Texas 77002

University of Houston
Ms. Susan Macy, Director (713) 752-8400
Small Business Development Center
601 Jefferson, Suite 2330
Houston, Texas 77002

Wharton County Junior College
Mr. Lynn Polson, Director (409) 532-2201
Small Business Development Center
Administration Building, Room 102
911 Boling Highway
Wharton, Texas 77488-0080

Northwestern Texas Small Business
Development Center
Mr. Craig Bean, Acting Region Director
(806) 745-3973 FAX: (806) 745-6207
TEXAS TECH UNIVERSITY: Center for Innovation
2579 South Loop 289, Suite 114
Lubbock, Texas 79423

Abilene Christian University
Mr. Stuart Hall, Director (915) 674-2776
Caruth Small Business Development Center
College of Business Administration
ACU Station, Box 8307
Abilene, Texas 79699

Midwestern State University
Mr. Tim Thomas, Director (817) 696-6738
Small Business Development Center
3400 Taft Boulevard
Wichita Falls, Texas 76308

Tarleton State University
Mr. Rusty Freed, Director (817) 968-9330
Small Business Development Center
College of Business Administration
Box T-158
Stephenville, Texas 76402

Texas Tech University
vacant (806) 745-1637
Small Business Development Center
Center for Innovation
2579 South Loop 289, Suite 210
Lubbock, Texas 79423

University of Texas/Permian Basin
Dr. Corbett Gaulden, Director (915) 563-0400
Small Business Development Center
4901 East University, Room 298
Odessa, Texas 79762

West Texas State University
Mr. Don Taylor, Director (806) 372-5151
Small Business Development Center
T. Boone Pickens School of Business
1800 South Washington, Suite 110
Amarillo, Texas 79102

South Texas Border Small Business
Development Center
Mr. Robert McKinley, Region Director
(512) 224-0791 FAX: (512) 222-9834
UNIVERSITY OF TEXAS AT SAN ANTONIO
College of Business
San Antonio, Texas 78249-0660

Angelo State University
Mr. Harlan Bruha, Director (915) 942-2098
Small Business Development Center
2610 West Avenue N: Campus Box 10910
San Angelo, Texas 76909

Corpus Christi Chamber of Commerce
Mr. Luiz Ortiz, Director (512) 882-6161
Small Business Development Center
1201 North Shoreline
Corpus Christi, Texas 78403

El Paso Community College
Mr. Roque R. Segura, Director
(915) 534-3410
Small Business Development Center
103 Montana Avenue, Room 202
El Paso, Texas 79902-3929

Kingsville Chamber of Commerce
Ms. Nancy Layser, Director
(512) 592-6438
Small Business Development Center
635 East King
Kingsville, Texas 78363

Laredo Development Foundation
Mr. Frank Leach, Director (512) 722-0563
Small Business Development Center
616 Leal Street
Laredo, Texas 78041

Texas Association of Mexican-American
Mr. Joe Morin, Director (512) 326-2256
Small Business Development Center
Chambers of Commerce
2211 South IH 35, Suite #103
Austin, Texas 78741

University of Houston-Victoria
Mr. Tom Murrah, Director (512) 575-8944
Small Business Development Center
700 Main Center, Suite 102
Victoria, Texas 77901

University of Texas-Pan American
Ms. Carminia Oris, Director (512) 381-3361
Small Business Development Center
1201 West University Drive
Edinburg, Texas 78539-2999

University of Texas at San Antonio
Mr. Morrison Woods, Director (512) 224-0791
Small Business Development Center
College of Business
San Antonio, Texas 78249-0660

UTAH

Utah Small Business Development Center
Mr. David A. Nimkin, Executive Director
(801) 581-7905 FAX: (801) 581-7814
UNIVERSITY OF UTAH
102 West 500 South, Suite 315
Salt Lake City, Utah 84101

Brigham Young University
Mr. Brent Petersen, Director (801) 378-4022
Small Business Development Center
School of Management
790 Tanner Building
Provo, Utah 84602

College of Eastern Utah
Mr. Nate McBride, Director (801) 637-1995
Small Business Development Center
451 East 400 North
Price, Utah 84501

Dixie College
Mr. Eric Pedersen, Director
(801) 673-4811
Small Business Development Center
225 South 700 East
St. George, Utah 84770

Snow College
Mr. Lynn Schiffman, Director
(801) 283-4021 or 283-6890
Small Business Development Center
345 West First North
Ephraim, Utah 84627

Southern Utah University
Mr. Ed Harris, Director (801) 586-5401
Small Business Development Center
351 West Center
Cedar City, Utah 84720

Utah State University
Mr. Franklin C. Prante, Director (801) 750-2277
Small Business Development Center
East Campus Building
Logan, Utah 84322-8330

Weber State College
Mr. Bruce Davis, Director (801) 626-7232
Small Business Development Center
School of Business and Economics
Ogden, Utah 84408-3806

VERMONT

Vermont Small Business Development Center
Mr. Norris Elliott, State Director
(802) 656-4479 FAX: (802) 656-8642
UNIVERSITY OF VERMONT:
Extension Service, Morrill Hall
Burlington, Vermont 05405-0106

Central Small Business Development Center
Ms. Lois Frey, Specialist (802) 888-4972
University of Vermont Extension Service
RFD One, Box 2280
Morrisville, Vermont 05661

NE Small Business Development Center
Mr. Edward Johnson, Specialist (802) 748-5512
University of Vermont Extension Service
HCR 31, Box 436
St. Johnsbury, Vermont 05819

NW Small Business Development Center
Mr. Phil Smith, Specialist (802) 655-9540
University of Vermont Extension Service
4A Laurette Drive
Winooski, Vermont 05404

SE Small Business Development Center
Mr. Norbert Johnston, Specialist (802) 257-7967
University of Vermont Extension Service
Resource Center
Box 2430: 411 Western Avenue
West Brattleboro, Vermont 05301

SW Small Business Development Center
Ms. Linda Aines, Specialist (802) 773-3349
University of Vermont Extension Service
Box 489
Rutland, Vermont 05701

VIRGINIA

Virginia Small Business Development Center
Dr. Robert Smith, State Coordinator
(804) 371-8258 FAX: (804) 371-8185
Commonwealth of Virginia
DEPARTMENT OF ECONOMIC DEVELOPMENT
1021 East Cary Street, 11th Floor
Richmond, Virginia 23219

Blue Ridge Small Business Development Center
Mr. John Jennings, Director (703) 983-0719
310 First Street, S.W. Mezzanine
Roanoke, Virginia 24011

Capital Area Small Business Development Center
Mr. Taylor Cousins, Director (804) 648-7838
801 East Main Street, Suite 501
Richmond, Virginia 23219

Central Virginia Small Business Development Center
Mr. Charles Kulp, Director (804) 295-8198
700 Harris Street, Suite 207
Charlottesville, Virginia 22901-4553

Flory Small Business Development Center
Ms. Linda Decker, Director (703) 335-2500
10311 Sudley Manor Drive
Manassas, Virginia 22110

James Madison University
Ms. Karen Wigginton, Director (703) 568-6334
Small Business Development Center
College of Business Building, Room 523
Harrisonburg, Virginia 22807

Longwood College
Mr. Gerald L. Hughes, Jr., Director (804) 395-2086
Small Business Development Center
Farmville, Virginia 23901

Longwood College
Mr. Carroll Thackston, Business Analyst
(804) 575-0044
South Boston Branch, 3403 Halifax Road
P.O. Box 739
South Boston, Virginia 24592

Lynchburg Small Business Development Center
Mr. Barry Lyons, Director (804) 582-6100
147 Mill Ridge Road
Lynchburg, Virginia 25402-4341

Mountain Empire Community College
Ms. Helen Duncan, Director (703) 523-2400
Small Business Development Center
Drawer 700, Route 23
Big Stone Gap, Virginia 24219

Northern Virginia Small Business
Development Center
Mr. Mike Kehoe, Director (703) 993-2131
4260 Chainbridge Road, Suite B-1
Fairfax, Virginia 22030

Small Business Development Center
of Hampton Roads, Inc.
Mr. William J. Holloran, Jr., Director
(804) 622-6414 or 825-2957
420 Bank Street: P.O. Box 327
Norfolk, Virginia 23501

Southwest Virginia Community College
Mr. R. Victor Brungart, Director (703) 964-7345
Small Business Development Center
P.O. Box SVCC
Richlands, Virginia 24641

WASHINGTON

Washington State Small Business
Development Center
Mr. Lyle M. Anderson, State Director
(509) 335-1576 FAX: (509) 335-0949
WASHINGTON STATE UNIVERSITY
College of Business and Economics
441 Todd Hall
Pullman, Washington 99164-4740

Bellevue Small Business Development Center
Mr. Bill Huenefeld, Director (206) 643-2888
13555 Bel-Red Road #208
Bellevue, Washington 98005

Big Bend Community College
Mr. Pat Tuohy, Director (509) 762-6289
Small Business Development Center
Building 1500
7662 Chanute Street
Moses Lake, Washington 98837-3299

Columbia Basin College
Mr. Glynn Lamberson, Director (509) 735-6222
Tri-Cities Small Business Development Center
901 North Colorado
Kennewick, Washington 99336

Columbia River Economic Development Council
Ms. Holli Baumunk, Director (206) 693-2555
Small Business Development Center
100 East Columbia Way
Vancouver, Washington 98660-3156

Department of Trade and Economic Development
Mr. Earl True, Business Dev. Specialist
(206) 586-4854
Business Assistance Center
Small Business Development Center
919 Lakeridge Way, Suite A
Olympia, Washington 98502

Edmonds Community College
Mr. Jack Wicks, Director (206) 745-0430
Small Business Development Center
917 134th Street, S.W.
Everett, Washington 98204

International Trade Institute
Ms. Halina Bojarski, IT Specialist
(206) 527-3733
North Seattle Community College
Small Business Development Center
9600 College Way North
Seattle, Washington 98103

Skagit Valley College
Mr. Peter Stroosma, Director (206) 428-1282
Small Business Development Center
2405 College Way
Mt. Vernon, Washington 98273

Small Business Development Center
Mr. Bill Jacobs, Director (206) 464-5450
2001 Sixth Avenue, Suite 2608
Seattle, Washington 98121-2518

Small Business Development Center
Ms. Ruth Ann Halford, Director (206) 764-5375
Duwamish Industrial Educational Center
6770 East Marginal Way South
Seattle, Washington 98108-1499

Small Business Development Center
Mr. Neil Delisanti, Director (206) 272-7232
300 Sea-First: Financial Center, 950 Pacific Avenue
Tacoma, Washington 98402

Small Business Development Center
Mr. George Buckner, Director (509) 662-8016
Grand Central Building: 25 North Wenatchee Avenue
Wenatchee, Washington 98801

Washington State University
Mr. Terry Cornelison, Director (509) 335-1576
Small Business Development Center
245 Todd Hall
Pullman, Washington 99164-4727

Washington State University-Spokane
Mr. John King, Director (509) 456-2781
Small Business Development Center
West 601 First Street
Spokane, Washington 99204-0399

Wenatchee Valley College
Mr. Ron Neilsen, Director (509) 826-5107
Small Business Development Center
P.O. Box 1042
Omak, Washington 98841

Western Washington University
Mr. Lynn Trzynka, Director (206) 676-3899
Small Business Development Center
College of Business and Economics
415 Parks Hall
Bellingham, Washington 98225

Yakima Valley Community College
Ms. Janice Durnil, Director (509) 575-2284
Small Business Development Center
P.O. Box 1647
Yakima, Washington 98907

WEST VIRGINIA

West Virginia Small Business Development Center
Ms. Eloise Jack, State Director
(304) 348-2960 FAX: (304) 348-0127
GOVERNOR'S OFFICE OF COMMUNITY
AND INDUSTRIAL DEVELOPMENT
1115 Virginia Street, East
Charleston, West Virginia 25310

Bluefield State College
Mr. Keith Zinn, Program Manager (304) 327-4107
Small Business Development Center
219 Rock Street
Bluefield, West Virginia 24701

Concord College
Mr. Greg Helbig, Program Manager (304) 384-5103
Small Business Development Center
Center for Economic Action: Box D-125
Athens, West Virginia 24712

Fairmount State College
Mr. Dale Bradley, Program Manager (304) 367-4125
Small Business Development Center
Fairmount, West Virginia 26554

Governor's Office of Community and
Industrial Development
Ms. Wanda Chenoweth, Program Manager
(304) 348-2960
Small Business Development Center
1115 Virginia Street,
East Charleston, West Virginia 25301

Marshall University
Ms. Elaine Hayslett, Program Manager
(304) 696-6789
Small Business Development Center
1050 Fourth Avenue
Huntington, West Virginia 25755-2126

Potomac State College
Ms. Sharon Butner, Program Manager
(304) 788-3011
Small Business Development Center
75 Arnold Street
Keyser, West Virginia 26726

Shepherd College
Mr. Fred Baer, Program Manager 800-344-5231
Small Business Development Center
120 North Princess Street
Shepherdstown, West Virginia 25443

West Virginia Institute of Technology
Mr. James Epling, Program Manager (304) 442-5501
Small Business Development Center
Room 102, Engineering Building
Montgomery, West Virginia 25136

West Virginia Northern Community College
Mr. Ed Huttenhower, Program Manager
(304) 233-5900
Small Business Development Center: College Square
Wheeling, West Virginia 26003

West Virginia University
Mr. Stan Kloc, Program Manager
(304) 293-5839
Small Business Development Center
P.O. Box 6025
Morgantown, West Virginia 26506

West Virginia University at Parkersburg
Mr. Barry Lyons, Program Manager
(304) 424-8277
Small Business Development Center
Route 5, Box 167-A
Parkersburg, West Virginia 26101

WISCONSIN

Wisconsin Small Business Development Center
Mr. William H. Pinkovitz, State Director
(608) 263-7794 FAX: (608) 262-3878
UNIVERSITY OF WISCONSIN
432 North Lake Street, Room 423
Madison, Wisconsin 53706

International Trade Program
Ms. Sandra Jahns, IT Specialist (608) 263-7810
University of Wisconsin: 423 North Lake Street
Madison, Wisconsin 53706
University of Wisconsin at Eau Claire

Mr. Fred Waedt, Director (715) 836-5811
Small Business Development Center
113 Schneider Hall
Eau Claire, Wisconsin 54701

University of Wisconsin at Green Bay
Mr. James Holly, Director (414) 465-2089
Small Business Development Center
2420 Nicolet Drive - 460 Wood Hall
Green Bay, Wisconsin 54311-7001

University of Wisconsin at La Crosse
Dr. A. William Pollman, Director (608) 785-8782
Small Business Development Center
School of Business Administration
La Crosse, Wisconsin 54601

University of Wisconsin at Madison
Ms. Joan Gillman, Director (608) 263-0221
Small Business Development Center
905 University Avenue
Madison, Wisconsin 53715

University of Wisconsin at Milwaukee
Ms. Ann Kates, Program Manager
(414) 224-3240
Small Business Development Center
929 North Sixth Street
Milwaukee, Wisconsin 53203

University of Wisconsin at Oshkosh
Mr. Richard Krueger, Director of Counseling
(414) 424-1541
Small Business Development Center
157 Clow Faculty Building
Oshkosh, Wisconsin 54901

University of Wisconsin at Parkside
Ms. Patricia Duetsch, Director of Counseling
(414) 553-2189
Small Business Development Center
234 Tallent Hall
Kenosha, Wisconsin 53141

University of Wisconsin at Stephens Point
Mr. Mark Stover, Director (715) 346-2004
Small Business Development Center
012 Old Main Building
Stevens Point, Wisconsin 54481

Wisconsin American Indian Economic Development
Mr. Gary Mejchar, Program Manager (715) 346-2004
University of Wisconsin at Stevens Point
Main Building
Stevens Point, Wisconsin 54481

University of Wisconsin at Superior
Mr. Neil Hensrud, Director (715) 394-8351
Small Business Development Center
29 Sundquist Hall
Superior, Wisconsin 54880

University of Wisconsin at Whitewater
Ms. Carla Lenk, Director (414) 472-3217
Small Business Development Center
2000 Carlson Building
Whitewater, Wisconsin 53190

Wisconsin Innovation Service Center
Ms. Debra Malewicki, Program Manager
(414) 472-1365
University of Wisconsin at Whitewater
402 McCutchan Hall
Whitewater, Wisconsin 53190

WIS-BID (Procurement Match Program)
Ms. Vicki Kalscheuer, WIS-BID Specialist
(414) 927-5484
W9859 Highway 16 and 60
Reeseville, Wisconsin 53579

WYOMING

Wyoming Small Business
Development Center
Mr. Jim Glover, State Director
(307) 235-4825 FAX: (307) 473-7243
CASPER COLLEGE:
111 West Second Street, Suite 416
Casper, Wyoming 82601

Casper College
Ms. Barbara Stuckert, Director
(307) 235-4827
Small Business Development Center
350 West "A" Street, Suite 200
Casper, Wyoming 82601

Central Wyoming College
Mr. Bruce Armentrout, Director
(307) 332-3394 800-735-8394
Small Business Development Center
360 Main Street
Lander, Wyoming 82520

Eastern Wyoming Community College
Mr. Jay Nielson, Director (307) 358-4090
Small Business Development Center
203 North Sixth Street
Douglas, Wyoming 82633

Laramie County Community College
Mr. Jim Lamprecht, Director (307) 778-1222
Small Business Development Center
1400 East College Drive
Cheyenne, Wyoming 82007

Northern Wyoming Community College District
Ms. Judith Semple, Director (307) 686-0297
Gillette Campus:
Small Business Development Center
720 West Eighth
Gillette, Wyoming 82716

Northwest Community College
Mr. Lloyd Snyder, Director (307) 754-3746
Small Business Development Center
146 South Bent #103
Powell, Wyoming 82435

University of Wyoming
Ms. Gail Mattheus, Director (307) 766-2363
Small Business Development Center
P.O. Box 3275
Laramie, Wyoming 82071

Western Wyoming Community College
Mr. Ron Johnson, Director (307) 382-1830
Small Business Development Center
P.O. Box 428
Rock Springs, Wyoming 82902

Index

Other JIST Publications for Entrepreneurs

Self-Employment: From Dream to Reality

An Interactive Workbook for Starting Your Small Business
by Linda D. Gilkerson & Theresia Paauweson

More money! More time with your family! More control over your life! Just some good reasons to start your own business. The authors show that most people can start a very small business with no previous business experience—and little money to invest.

ISBN: 1-56370-443-9 ☆ **$16.95** ☆ Order Code: J4439

Franchise Opportunities Handbook

A Complete Guide for People Who Want to Start Their Own Franchise
by U.S. Department of Commerce & LaVerne Ludden, ED.D.

Based on the latest data from the U.S. Department of Commerce, this 23rd Edition gives helpful advice on selecting a franchise and starting a business. The most comprehensive resource of its kind—more than 1,500 listings!

ISBN 1-57112-073-4 ☆ **$16.95** ☆ Order Code: P0734

Be Your Own Business!

The Definitive Guide to Entrepreneurial Success
Edited by Marcia R. Fox, PH.D.

Millions of Americans dream about starting their own business, but don't know where to begin. The information in *Be Your Own Business!* can help readers make all the right choices at every step along the road to becoming successful entrepreneurs.

ISBN 1-57112-082-3 ☆ **$16.95** ☆ Order Code P0823

Home but Not Alone

The Parents' Work-at-Home Handbook
by Katherine Murray

Start a home-based enterprise and open the door to a rewarding and challenging new lifestyle for you—and your family. Includes everything to make your transition to self-employment easier and more rewarding!

ISBN 1-57112-080-7 ☆ **$14.95** ☆ Order Code P0807